NATURALLY THIN KIDS

*How to Protect Your Kids
from Obesity and Eating Disorders for Life*

by
Jean Antonello, RN, BSN,

author of
HOW TO BECOME NATURALLY THIN BY EATING MORE
and
BREAKING OUT OF FOOD JAIL

Naturally Thin Kids

© 2005 by Jean Antonello

Published by the Heartland Book Company
3013 13th Terrace NW
New Brighton, MN 55112
ISBN 0-9625351-9-2

Cover and text design by Garborg Design Works

Printed in the United States of America by the artisans at Bethany Press International

Other books by Jean Antonello:
How to be Naturally Thin by Eating More, and
Breaking Out of Food Jail

For more information please visit the website:
www.naturally-thin.com

To my kids, Michael, Genevieve and Joe

I especially grateful to the scientists who have contributed significantly to our growing understanding of obesity: Thomas A. Wadden, PhD, Kelly D. Brownell, PhD, A.J. Stuntgard, MD, Adam Drenowski, PhD, James Rippe, MD, and Aaron Altschul, as well as many other workers in this field. The principles of *Naturally Thin Kids* emerged along the path that these pioneers have cleared.

I also appreciate the many moms and dads who generously shared their knowledge, concerns, questions and experiences with me.

Thanks also to my professional friends for their work on the book: editor Joyce Ellis, distributor Joyce Hart, designer Chris Garborg, and coordinator Mike Beard.

Most of all I thank my husband, Michael, for his encouragement and support.

Train up a child in the way he should go,
and when he is old he will not depart from it.

Proverbs 22:6

CONTENTS

Introduction

You're reading this book because you care—about your kids' health, about their appearance, about their self-esteem, and about their social lives. You want to help them to want to eat well, to have attractive bodies, to enjoy food (good food!) without all the anxiety and confusion of our culture.

Recent statistics suggest that one in four children between six and seventeen is overweight. Some say one in three. Overweight young people are extremely likely to suffer from lifelong weight, eating, and health struggles, not to mention the social rejection and isolation the obese often experience. Although we are worried, many of us are too confused ourselves to know what to do to help our kids.

With combined pressures to be ever thinner and an overabundance of contradictory diet and nutrition information, children, adolescents and parents in the U.S. are confused about what, when, and how much they should eat. The flood of "eat less" diet messages of our culture is bound to affect their eating—and it does. As a result, many kids lose touch with their own bodies—with their natural eating instincts—making them vulnerable to weight and eating struggles.

Most kids are more afraid of being fat than of jeopardizing their growth with poor nutrition. Statistics show alarming increases in eating disorders among young teens. Once rare, these conditions are becoming much more commonplace among adolescents and even children. And weight problems among youth have doubled in the past three decades, according to obesity researchers.

Where is all this eating confusion and trouble coming from? What exactly are our families and our weight-obsessed culture teaching kids about eating and weight that are so unhelpful, even destructive? And why are more and more children plagued with excess weight and eating disorders? Is it stress or peer pressure? Is it high-fat foods? Fashion trends? Do kids have more emotional problems nowadays? Is television to blame? Fast food? Inadequate exercise?

Oddly, our dietary guidelines and weight-loss ideas are notoriously inconsistent, even contradictory. Today's recommendations and rules could easily become tomorrow's stand-up comedy material. Ironically, traditional dieting actually promotes obesity and eating disorders! This is a crucial fact and foundational principle of *Naturally Thin Kids.*

We want our kids to be free of the strain of obsessive dieting, to be able to enjoy eating like normal people. And we can. By changing the patterns that lead to eating and weight troubles, we can get our kids back to natural, healthful eating. These are the "how-to" issues this book addresses.

Our worries are realistic

Remedies for weight and eating disturbances have been remarkably unsuccessful for adults as well as children. There seems to be almost no hope for most adults trapped by weight and eating struggles, which often last a lifetime. Obesity has a long-term cure rate of less than 5 percent and some medical professionals consider eating disorders more difficult to cure than drug addition.

Naturally Thin Kids is not a diet book but a path to prevention. This path is very much needed. People with life-long struggles with weight and eating problems abound. For example, now forty-six, Suzanne talks about her earliest attempts to control her weight in junior high school. She was just chubby then, she says, but already self-conscious about her changing body. Once she started dieting, however, her appetite and her weight and her life were never normal again. After thirty-four years of battling her appetite and eating behavior by nearly very means imaginable, today Suzanne carries 240 pounds on her five foot three inch frame. In addition to the self-esteem and social struggles she has faced for years, she is now beginning to have medical consequences as well. Stories like Suzanne's are all too common and not likely to change soon. And most "Suzannes" of our generation now have children of their own and don't know how to help them avoid the same debilitating struggles. We certainly need to approach eating and weight problems from a different angle—prevention. We must teach children to eat and live in ways that insure their optimal body weight and healthful eating habits.

Why hasn't this happened yet? Why isn't the low-fat diet plus more exercise emphasis working? Something is missing—some basic information that our kids need to know in order to keep them free from excess weight and eating problems. This missing piece is what *Naturally Thin Kids* is about.

Although physiological causes for weight and eating problems are basically the same in adults, teens, and children, food availability and eating patterns create some important distinctions among different age groups.

What's special about kids?

Adults are generally in control of their own diets and are capable of making their own adjustments in their food selection and eating behavior, for better or worse. Kids, on the other hand, have only limited power over what and when they eat. Their parents and caregivers usually provide the food and drink they consume and decide when and what and even how much they eat. They may even counsel kids about their diets.

Because the eating environment of children is generally created for them in this way, *Naturally Thin Kids* is written for anyone in charge of making available to kids food, drink, and information about eating. This book aims to provide the basic principles of natural leanness to help parents confidently grocery shop, cook, pack lunches, and advise their kids about healthful eating.

There are also problems peculiar to children's eating, including school and sports schedules, school menus, school time food availability, finicky appetites, quality of food preparation and overall availability, food allergies, childhood illness, kids' activity (and inactivity) levels, erratic hunger in children and teens, after-school program snacks, or home-alone snack times, and growth spurts. These and other kid features, including their basic immaturity, make teaching kids positive lifelong eating habits a real challenge.

Parents need specific information about these special kid issues—new information. *Naturally Thin Kids* provides this new knowledge—including many facts that will surprise you. Armed with these insights, you can help your child maintain a healthy weight and enjoy a natural relationship with food—for life.

Naturally Thin Kids focuses on *when* kids eat—kids eating good food *at the right time*. This "timing" piece makes all the difference in preventing, and even treating, eating and weight problems in kids. The simplistic approach of other books on kids' weight problems—exercise more and eat a lower fat diet—is not only doomed to fail for most kids, but it actually contributes to unhealthy eating patterns and weight problems!

This timing principle, missing in the traditional diet approach, is the key to lasting success for kids and adults who want to eat normally and maintain a healthy body weight. Timing is the key to kids' natural leanness. Understanding this fact will enable you to confidently help your kids develop healthful eating habits. This insight, along with some nutrition information, will help you know how to handle each situation that comes up with your child because these unchanging guidelines spring from simple physiology.

But why should we have to teach our kids about eating—about this "timing" thing? Although babies and young children instinctively eat "on demand," and the "timing" of their eating is natural, our lifestyle and beliefs gradually interfere with normal, instinctive, eating. These interfering influences include the schedules kids are on, society's prejudices about eating and obesity, and the types of foods available for kids to eat.

Three Landmarks

Clearly, parents are challenged by these distractions to natural eating. But there is a very simple roadmap for them to follow to help them get their kids back to natural eating behavior. *Naturally Thin Kids* fills in the details of the map.

Here are the three crucial issues the book covers:

1. when kids' bodies need food
2. what food their bodies need and why
3. what happens when their bodies don't get what they need.

Without this information, even the most determined and conscientious caregivers are doomed to fail in their goal of supporting healthy eating in their kids. And failure in this area certainly makes kids more vulnerable to weight problems and eating struggles throughout their lives.

You will need patience—with yourself and with your kids—and perseverance, too. Lasting changes usually take a while to lock into place, but this is a plan you and your kids can comfortably live with for the rest of your lives: simple, workable, realistic and practical. Get ready to learn fascinating and effective new ways to prevent serious lifelong struggles for your children!

Part One:

Why Do Kids Develop Weight Problems?

Ignoring Hunger

1

Kids can learn that their bodies are wonderfully designed to regulate food intake and weight.

Only an hour after my son Joe was born, I heard a faint, high-pitched squeaking noise in our hospital room. Perhaps it was the exhaustion of labor and birth, but I was convinced for a moment that there was a little mouse squeaking on the floor under my bed. Finally, I looked around and followed the sound right to the bassinet. Tiny, newborn Joe was sucking hungrily on his fist.

Human beings are natural-born eaters. The instinct to seek and eat food under the influence of hunger is a trait we share with the whole animal kingdom. Fortunately, it is a powerful instinct. Unfortunately, we are the "animals" who can make choices that violate our instinctive drive for food. This intellectual ability makes us supremely vulnerable to weight and eating problems. Did you know that there is no obesity among animals in the wild? This is not a simple consequence of high activity levels as animals seek food. It is also the consequence of instinctive eating.

What instinctive eating looks like

If you have ever cared for a baby or small child, you have probably seen instinctive eating in action. It is very uncomplicated. Hunger is actually a form of pain or distress that can only be relieved by one thing: food. So, when babies or little kids grow hungry, they tell you, one way or another. They automatically communicate distress or seek food when hunger strikes.

Babies instinctively cry, which alerts a parent or caregiver. Older kids who are mobile may help themselves to the cupboard or refrigerator. Little kids don't think about their hunger. When they get hungry they naturally try to get food.

The hunger-induced distress goes away when young children are satisfied, and they stop eating. Their bodies will regulate the amount of food they eat unless someone interferes. Most parents and caregivers usually let children eat as much as they want, confident that they will automatically stop when they have had enough. (Isn't this interesting?) The same instinct that drives these little kids to seek food also determines how much food they will eat. Kids don't have to think about this either. When kids feel full, as most parents know, it is virtually impossible to get them to eat any more—of anything!

Every person who has fed a baby knows what this looks like. The baby is cooing and reaching for the spoonful of tasty applesauce for, say, the first eight bites. Then, without much warning, the spoonful goes in and—squirt—the baby pushes it right out again. It dribbles down the chin in a rather disgusting way, and the feeder usually scoops it off the baby's face and right back into the mouth.

This recycling game may work one time, maybe two, but after that the baby will not allow one spoonful more into its tightly pursed lips, no matter how much the feeder may persist. The baby is full and its little body knows it without any outside information or control.

New moms and dads are surprised and sometimes frustrated when their babies take a full bottle of formula at one feeding and only a half bottle at the next. This is a good case for breast-feeding. No one really knows how much the baby is actually getting, so there's less anxiety. Sometimes a hungry toddler is satisfied with only a few bites of an apple. And other times this same child may down three bowls of cereal in quick succession.

Instinctive eating in kids often is *not* regular or predictable. It happens. Hunger happens and fullness happens, as long as we allow kids to eat freely.

Young kids' bodies naturally take charge of their fuel needs, designed to perfectly regulate energy intake and output.

Most babies and small children are just the right size because of these biological regulators. But what happens when kids are not the right size—when they are too fat? Is there a malfunction in their energy regulators, or what?

Once in a great while there is a biological malfunction, but almost always, little kids who get too fat are out of touch with their natural eating instincts. For some reason or another, they've stopped eating according to their bodies' signals at times, and this causes trouble:
- food quantity trouble
- food quality trouble and
- food craving trouble.

Ultimately all this can lead to weight trouble. And weight trouble almost always leads to yet more eating problems.

We tend, as a culture, to see natural eating instincts as something of an odd biological-mechanical failure for many people, including children. We think of our own, and our kids' eating instincts, as corrupt. They can't be trusted. So, we don't trust them. We ignore our own hunger at times, even chronically, especially if we are overweight. We think it is perfectly fine for our kids to go hungry, too, once they are past the age where unsatisfied hunger makes them cry.

Of course we don't usually starve our kids willfully, but missed breakfasts, snack-like lunches on the run, and complaints of "still hungry" after eating are usually unremarkable events in our everyday lives. Don't we think, at some level, that going hungry is normal, even healthy, for kids now and then? Don't we think it's actually good for them in a way, to go without food, to, say, build character? Aren't we afraid that if they don't learn to go hungry sometimes, they may become fat? So, we teach our kids to ignore their hunger, either subtly or directly.

Eating is *meant* to be instinctive (based on hunger and fullness signals). That's the way we all start out. But kids get out of touch with these natural patterns for various reasons. For instance, what happens when we overrule our kids' eating instincts (hunger) based on our "knowledge" and the restrictions of our own obesity fears and fast-paced lifestyle? And what happens when kids can't eat instinctively because their hunger comes when there is no food around? Are all kids affected the same in these situations or are the consequences for these changes worse for some kids than for others?

The answers to these questions are coming up. When we discover that eating restrictions are a big part of the problem, we can keep instinctive eaters on track and help other kids get back to more natural, instinctive eating habits.

Instinctive eating threatened
Adolescent Awareness: Genevieve's Story

My daughter, Genevieve, was a blooming thirteen years old when she came to me one day, complaining that she had gone from size 5 pants to size 9—in about six months! I hadn't noticed that she cared about her size before this, but she was obviously alarmed now.

"Mom, you have to teach me what you teach people in your seminars about being naturally thin," she begged. "I just keep getting bigger. What can I do so I don't get fat?"

Because she was obviously in an adolescent growth spurt, I wasn't alarmed about Genevieve's "sudden" size increase. She didn't look fat and, although she had some new padding around her middle, I considered that normal for her age—a temporary "bloom" of young womanhood. However, that same bloom had caused such a panic in me at age thirteen that I had reacted by dieting and fighting my body, and hating it, for nearly twenty years. So, I was worried about Genevieve's alarm, concerned that she was vulnerable to the same diet trap I had fallen into thirty years before.

Genevieve's real crisis was her fear,
which caused her to stop trusting her body.

Weight gain, especially the relatively rapid weight gain during puberty in girls, can cause anxiety and even panic in young adolescents. Genevieve was beginning to worry that her body was out of control and that she couldn't trust her appetite anymore. For the first time in her life, she had become aware of the amount of food she was eating, and she began to watch what other, thinner girls were eating. She had never talked about dieting with her friends before. The subject had bored her. But now she began to listen as they shared the latest weight-loss ideas. Fortunately, Genevieve never actually started a diet herself, but she did try to cut back on her lunches. And she ignored her intense hunger during hockey practice instead of getting a snack.

Children must never abandon instinctive (body-controlled) eating if they want to avoid obesity and eating disorders. Genevieve was on the verge of doing just that—consciously abandoning her natural eating instincts in order to control her weight gain. And she, like all adolescents, had absolutely no idea how dangerous her "solution" really was.

Before traveling too far down that road, Genevieve learned new information about her body that allayed her fears and showed her why she must stay in tune with her natural eating instincts. I coached Genevieve in the *Naturally Thin* principles (outlined in my first books), and she discovered that staying in touch with her natural appetite and eating good-quality food whenever she got hungry would normalize her appetite and stabilize her weight at the best place for her. Applying the principles with discipline, she carefully avoided going hungry and ate only good-quality food. Genevieve found that she could trust her body if she focused on eating well.

If she had given up her natural, instinctive eating patterns, she would have shifted the main control for her eating behavior from her body signals to her own ideas of what, when, and how much she should eat. This would have made her extremely vulnerable to developing both weight and eating problems from that day forward—maybe forever.

It is this shift away from instinctive, natural eating behavior that contributes most powerfully to kids' weight and eating problems. It can happen consciously (based on a decision that a kid makes, as it nearly did in Genevieve's case), or it can also happen without the kid's awareness or intention.

What other factors cause the shift away from instinctive eating?

Genevieve is a good example of how multitudes of teenage and even preteen girls consciously start fighting their bodies' normal need for food, *because of fear.* But many kids unconsciously control their eating, unaware of their fears about their changing body shape. And sometimes a parent, because of anxiety, rigid expectations or ignorance, (especially if a child becomes overweight), assumes control for a child's diet, overriding the child's natural eating patterns. Many of these parents, overweight themselves, are afraid that their child will suffer the same struggle if the parents don't intervene.

Often no one actually disrupts instinctive eating. It simply becomes impossible for kids to stay in touch with their bodies because of poor food availability. A hungry body can't be well satisfied when the refrigerator or cupboards only store unhealthy food choices. In many situations, such as after school practices, kids have no food available at all. Even when food is present in vending machines, for example, many kids don't carry adequate money to buy it.

It doesn't matter to bodies what interferes with the food supply. The effects are the same. Whenever bodies don't get good food at the right time, the control of food intake shifts away from the body. Bodies aren't built to figure out why. They're built to adapt.

These are the three basic ways kids lose touch with their bodies' natural, instinctive eating patterns:

1. Children or adolescents themselves start to consciously or unconsciously interfere with their normal eating instincts for various reasons (fear, athletics).

2. Parents or caregivers consciously or unconsciously interfere with kids' eating and/or food availability.

3. Food availability is not adequate, either quantitatively (not enough food for hungry kids) or qualitatively (not enough good quality food), or both.

The third trouble area, inadequate food availability, is rarely deliberate (except in the case of adults trying to get over-weight kids to eat less). More often it is caused by schedule conflicts, time constraints, and inadequate knowledge about food quality. For example, there isn't time to eat a decent breakfast, or soccer practice starts right after school with no time for a snack. School lunch may be served at 12:45, almost six hours after breakfast and long after hunger has set in.

But whatever causes kids to lose touch with their natural eating instincts, we can prevent kids' eating and weight problems by getting them back in touch with their bodies' instinctive eating patterns.

Fortunately, Genevieve talked to me before she started dieting or making any concerted effort to control her eating and weight. She didn't skip meals or try to restrict her eating too much. But there were areas where she needed to make some adjustments and get back in touch with her body signals.

The information I shared with her reassured her that her body was doing just fine, and she needed to cooperate with it instead of fighting it. She simply needed to avoid going hungry and choose good quality foods. Genevieve was perhaps the best student I ever coached. She did everything I told her to do, and it paid off. She was motivated and had confidence in what I said, but I couldn't have done it for her. I simply showed her the path.

Parents (and others who care) can help their kids get on the path, too, with the information and support in this book. The path is paved with simple principles that can be applied to children's dietary habits not for a few weeks or months, but for a lifetime of healthy eating.

The principle behind instinctive eating patterns: Adaptation

When Genevieve asked, "What can I do so I don't get fat?", I began by teaching her about a simple concept known as the Theory of Adaptation. This concept explains why dieting backfires and why, physiologically, fighting natural eating instincts causes humans to struggle with their eating and weight. It also shows how the body's survival needs affect eating behavior.

I had discovered fourteen years earlier that weight and eating problems were much more complicated than simply too much food and/or too little exercise. Although these things are important, they are not single-handedly responsible. I knew Genevieve's struggle could only be solved and these potential problems prevented by teaching her how her body works. Her understanding of and cooperation with her body were the keys to her success.

The idea behind Adaptation is that human bodies of any age can adjust to changes in their surroundings—adapt to different environments in order to survive. When we say that children's bodies are adaptive, it means they can make internal adjustments in response to changes in the environment. These adjustments are not conscious or voluntary. They are automatic.

One familiar example of adaptation is muscle development. As muscles are used more, they grow bigger and stronger. When muscles are not used, they shrink and become weaker. This is known as the principle of use and disuse. When young Tommy has the cast removed from his arm after six weeks, he exclaims, "Mom! My arm looks dead! And it feels dead too!" The injured limb is weaker and smaller compared to the uninjured one.

Another example of adaptation is body hydration or fluid balance. Human bodies are equipped with special hormones and sensors that recirculate water when a person doesn't drink enough fluids. The main hormone that regulates this is called the antidiuretic hormone because it prevents diuresis or fluid loss through the kidneys. Then, when she starts to drink more fluids, the body senses this, the antidiuretic hormone level falls, and the body begins to eliminate the excess water so it doesn't get overloaded.

And if she is constantly underhydrated—never drinking enough—her body recirculates extra fluid all the time, retaining fluid, because of the continuous need. This is why doctors tell their patients who retain fluid to drink more water. These adaptive mechanisms support survival, because dehydration is very hard on a body. In extreme cases it can even cause death. Because of their lower fluid volume, children are even more vulnerable to dehydration than adults, although they have the same basic protective mechanisms.

So what?

When I explained adaptation to Genevieve, she understood what I was saying but still wanted to know specifically how to stop her body from getting fat. And you may wonder too: What has adaptation got to do with preventing kids' eating and weight problems?

Hold on, we're getting there. Let's look at one more area of adaptation so that all this can start to make sense.

Besides the examples of muscle use/disuse, and water intake, bodies also adapt to the food supply—to whether or not they get enough good food when they need it. Variations in the food supply, like fluid availability, force bodies to adjust internally to keep going. These internal adjustments (adaptations), influence eating behavior. In order to help kids avoid eating and weight problems, it's crucial to understand how this works.

How bodies adapt to variations in the food supply

The urge to eat food when we get hungry is, in fact, a survival instinct. That's why it's so powerful. But throughout history the food supply for humans has often been uncertain, and human bodies have needed ways of adjusting to food shortages.

OK, but how do our bodies do that? Just as the underhydrated body retains water to protect itself from dangerous dehydration, the underfed body conserves energy and "retains" food—in the form of fat—to protect itself from starvation. Fat is simply extra food stored on the body, and it is crucial for a body that is underfed at times to retain extra fat. This is how our bodies are designed.

But aren't underfed people skinny—like the starving people in poor countries? They don't have any extra fat!

These people are chronically underfed. That's different. In order to adapt to periods of famine (undereating) by storing extra food, bodies need more than enough food some of the time. In other words, the undereating can't be constant or the body won't have any extra food from which to store extra fat. But when typical Americans don't get enough food to eat some of the time (but at other times have plenty), they overeat to compensate, and their bodies store extra fat as an adaptation.

Just as the trigger for fluid retention is "underdrinking," the trigger for the extra fat storage is the "undereating," the temporary "famine adaptation." This is very important to remember. The actual fat storage is accomplished by compensatory overeating and other internally controlled mechanisms.

Kids' bodies adapt to the availability of food exactly as adults do. When kids go hungry, (whether daily, weekly or occasionally), their bodies "learn" that survival depends on conserving energy and storing fat. The amount of extra fat depends on individual heredity and how long and serious the famines are. (More on these things later.) During famine times, or periods of undereating, there may or may not be noticeable changes in a child or teen. Weight may be fairly stable, but inside the child's body, all kinds of important adjustments are taking place. These adjustments are a body's ways of adapting to intermittent famines.

How kids' bodies adapt to going hungry

1. Decrease in metabolism. The rate that kids burn calories decreases to conserve energy.
2. Increase in appetite. Kids who miss meals or eat too little usually become extremely hungry.
3. Cravings for sweets and fats. Overhungry kids focus on rich foods for their "make-up eating."
4. Irritability and preoccupation with food. Kids nagging about food or "always hungry" are often actually underfed.
5. Avoidance of activity. Overhungry kids often don't feel like moving around.

Five adaptive responses that can be interpreted as symptoms of unsatisfied or undersatisfied hunger

These biological responses automatically happen to some degree when kids go hungry—no matter what the reason.

It could be sickness. Mary Ellen had her tonsils out when she was nine, after a string of infections the month before her surgery. She had a very poor appetite during this time and could only eat small amounts of soft food. She lost four pounds and her parents became alarmed at her increasingly thin appearance.

Or it could be time pressures. Maybe there's no time for breakfast. This happens a lot. Richard, father of three, complains that mornings are the worst time for trying to get a meal in. Everyone is rushing around, trying to get ready for school or work.

Or kids say they're not hungry when a meal is available. Then, when hunger strikes—maybe during classes or a sport practice—there's no food around. "I can't eat in the morning," fourteen-year-old Zack protests. "I'm just not hungry then! But by about 9:30 or 10 o'clock, I'm absolutely starving!" That's the beginning of third hour and there's no eating allowed in class or between classes.

These situations are often viewed as *problems with the child's body that adults need to fix.* As long as we keep trying fix eating and weight problems by treating the symptoms of poor eating patterns, we are doomed to fail. In fact, we are making matters worse for kids.

James, an overweight twelve-year-old, whose metabolic rate is adaptively low because of his erratic eating schedule and poor diet, is put on an exercise regimen to stimulate his sluggish metabolism. Consequently, James experiences even more severe famines because of his increased need for calories. And this ultimately leads to weight gain.

Mary, only four, has a raging sweet tooth. She is often indulged with sweets instead of better food offered more often.

Because of their enlarged appetites, kids who regularly miss meals super-size their fast foods (right along with their overhungry parents), and society blames the fast-food chains. Overhungry children or adolescents who complain about their excessive hunger may be ridiculed or ignored by their misunderstanding caretakers, especially if they are overweight. And no one ever suspects that chubby fifteen-year-old twins Tracy and Alice prefer being couch potatoes simply because they are dieting most of the time and not getting enough good food to provide the energy necessary for more physical activity.

The five adaptations in the above list may lead to weight gain and/or disturbed eating patterns in sensitive kids. Most still don't develop weight and eating problems during their first decade of life. But they develop *patterns of eating that put them at risk for these struggles by the time they are adolescents or young adults.* Kids are getting caught up in our eating-avoidance, diet-crazed culture, and most are eating recklessly out of ignorance. So more and more of them are developing weight and eating problems at an earlier age. This explains why a growing number of kids, the more biologically sensitive ones, are getting fat in childhood.

So how can we prevent these growing threats? Let's look in more detail at how going hungry and undereating affect kids.

Adaptation #1: Decrease in metabolic rate

Children's metabolic rates drop when they don't eat enough because their bodies must conserve energy during those times. In a real emergency situation when food becomes scarce or unavailable for a time, it is crucial for the body to "slow down its motor" in order to survive. This depression of metabolic rate in response to undereating can contribute significantly to weight gain. It also explains why some kids, who appear to eat no more (or even less) food than their peers, can plateau at a higher weight and/or gain weight.

There are two main ways to stimulate the metabolic rate: physical activity and eating. Most of us know that exercise is an effective way to raise the metabolism, but few people realize that eating stimulates metabolism too. The body can run at optimal energy output when it gets plenty of good fuel. There's no need to conserve.

But if there isn't enough fuel coming in, a child's body must become very efficient in its fuel use, burning calories sparingly until fuel becomes plentiful again. It's automatic.

It's important to remember that a child's body will slow down metabolically, based on a particular eating behavior, not on how much food is available. Children might live inside a grocery store, but if they don't eat enough or often enough, their metabolic rates will be lower than kids who generally eat freely whenever they are hungry.

Bear in mind that definite genetic variations in metabolic rate occur, and children, even from the same family, may have very different metabolisms. But eating behavior significantly influences metabolic rate, no matter what the genetics are, because of the influence of adaptation. We'll discuss these factors more in Chapter 3.

Adaptation #2: Increase in appetite

When kids begin eating long past the time they get hungry, (I call this "delayed eating"), hunger is likely excessive. Then eating and food choices get excessive too. Kids may say they're "starving," act out, or become obnoxious or irritable. These symptoms of low blood sugar are common in overhungry kids.

Ironically, kids who are the most demanding when they get hungry are often less vulnerable to weight and eating problems. The kids who seem to tolerate being hungry for longer periods of time are often more vulnerable to excessive weight gain. (More on this connection in Chapter 3.)

To further complicate this issue for caregivers, sometimes hunger fades when kids don't eat right away. This form of adaptation can be a problem too because their bodies tap their energy reserves for the fuel-release mechanisms normally reserved for occasional emergency situations. This causes a lot of internal stress, especially when kids are physically active. There'll be much more on these vital relationships in Chapter 2.

Adaptation #3: Cravings for sweets and fats

When kids don't eat as soon as they get hungry, or when they eat too little, they tend to want richer foods, more fatty foods, and sweets. These craving changes allow their bodies to make up for missed calories, promoting the consumption of quick but excess calories for fat storage. I call this "make-up eating." Remember, bodies that don't get enough food at times tend to store excess fat. This is how high-fat fast foods and snacks, such as cookies, brownies, ice cream, candy bars, and potato chips, can play a big role in kids' weight problems.

The high availability of these foods, and the strong urge to choose them over more healthful foods because of reckless eating patterns, adds up to trouble. The tendency to demand rich and sweet foods is a universal adaptation in kids who periodically undereat.

Does this mean that all the children who love candy (and that would be all children I have ever known) are adapting to famines? No. Many children, as well as adults, have a natural affinity for sweets that doesn't necessarily indicate an inadequate diet. Kids' preferences for sweets probably reflect their instinctive attraction to easy-to-digest carbohydrates such as fruits and honey. (Breast milk is sweet too.) If fruit and honey were the only sweet foods available to satisfy these cravings, we probably wouldn't be in nearly as much trouble as we are!

Adaptation #4: Irritability and preoccupation with food

Hungry people tend to become crabby and preoccupied with food. But going hungry affects children even more dramatically, perhaps because their bodies are less resilient under the stress of hunger. Their preoccupation with food is not a "psychological problem."

It makes no difference whether the kids are normal weight, overweight, or downright skinny. Irritability and preoccupation with food are signals that kids' bodies are in trouble. They need food and they need it now. Kids can wear almost anyone down with whining, crying, complaints, or even tantrums, when they are very hungry. Kids' irritability and preoccupation with food reflects their bodies' prioritizing food intake. It's all about survival.

Adaptation #5: Avoidance of activity

When children regularly go hungry, their bodies' survival instincts keep them from wasting energy in unnecessary physical activity. Hungry children can and will perform physically, but usually only when they feel they must because of an athletic event or a situation in which pride is involved. Hungry kids usually do not feel like moving around much. They may become lethargic and even act depressed and irritable. It isn't adaptive for kids who routinely go hungry to be active. So they often aren't.

The trouble is, many kids who experience "famine" regularly are actually overweight to some degree. Their inactivity looks like the cause of their weight problem, but again, it is only a symptom of adaptation. And then there are kids who are athletic and fat, too. This suggests that exercise is not the solution for kids' weight struggles. We need to correct their eating patterns. That's the bottom line.

Is this the whole story?

Does all this imply that going hungry is the single cause for kids' weight and eating problems? Of course it's not that simple. Food quality and physical activity play a role as well. But ignoring hunger—the famine experience—whatever the reason, whether conscious or accidental, is a huge piece in the puzzle. And this crucial piece has generally been ignored.

Experts who try to help overweight kids focus on low-fat diets with behavior modification, along with dramatically increased exercise regimens, fail most of the time. Research with adults who approach these problems with this formula has cast strong doubts on its lasting effectiveness. Like adults, kids who lose weight on these programs often require heavy monitoring to keep them compliant. How well do these approaches work in highly motivated adults without supervision? About 2 or 3 percent are considered successful, keeping off weight loss for five years. No statistics are available regarding children. But are they likely to do better than grown-ups?

What are we missing in the eat-less, exercise-more formula? We're missing the most powerful physical force in our kids' bodies: the survival instinct. If our approach to their eating and weight health continues to ignore this important piece, we won't likely rescue them from obesity and disturbed eating patterns. We must integrate this foundational concept in order to save them from an unending struggle with food issues, unhappiness, and physical complications.

To review: Going hungry or undereating some of the time are signals to a kid's body that it must adapt. Lack of food threatens survival, and all bodies are built to handle these threats via internal adaptations. When kids' hunger is ignored or undersatisfied, their bodies adapt in five ways in order to stay alive and healthy: decreased metabolism, increased appetite, cravings for sweets and rich foods, preoccupation with food, and avoidance of activity.

It's important to understand these five adaptive responses or symptoms that warn us of problems in our kids' eating behavior. But some obvious symptoms, such as excessive hunger and cravings, can be normal for kids at various stages of development. We'll be discussing these situations in later chapters, too.

The happy ending

I taught Genevieve the principles of adaptation and showed her how to eat instinctively to stay naturally slim ten years ago. Genevieve is twenty-four now—slim and happy, and eating! She has never been on a diet. She wasn't really cured of anything. She was never "fat" or troubled with an eating disorder. She was rescued in advance—saved forever from the struggles of obesity, artificial weight control and endless dieting because she learned how to cooperate with her body's natural eating instincts.

I have thought many times since Genevieve's request years ago about what might have happened to her if I hadn't known what to say—if I had had no answer for her. What if I'd still been dieting myself, struggling against my body's hunger and still trying to burn calories by exercising? It's a frightening thought, but I probably would have suggested a diet—some calorie restriction along with regular exercise. This may sound quite harmless to you now, but I hope that by the time you finish reading this book the idea horrifies you. I lost nearly two decades of my life to the diet lifestyle, and the notion that I might well have doomed my daughter to the same purgatory is truly frightening. In fact, it inspired me to write this book.

BAD

TIMING

2

When kids eat affects their food choices and portions.

Three facts explain how we have gotten into so much trouble with our eating and why kids are so vulnerable to developing eating and weight problems:

1. Going hungry on a regular basis sets up kids to develop weight and eating struggles sooner or later.
2. Kids ignoring hunger signals and waiting to eat seems rather benign and common, so no one has seen it as an important contributor to weight and eating problems in kids.
3. Delaying eating for significant periods of time usually has no obvious, immediate consequences.

Add to the mix our diet-obsessed and thinness-crazed culture, and you've got quite a stew of trouble brewing. How *can* something so simple as kids' eating patterns have such serious consequences? The answer concerns the *adaptive potential* human beings have developed over time—the ability of kids' bodies to survive famines.

The famine trigger

When a child or adolescent goes hungry for any reason, it can be accurately called a famine. For kids, regular famine experiences cause physiological changes (the five adaptive responses in Chapter 1) to support survival, but they backfire when we get caught in the trap of trying to fix the symptoms instead of solving the problem.

In order to prevent eating and weight problems, we must target the famine experience and understand its link to these adaptive responses. Eliminate the famines—both quality and quantity famines—and kids will become almost immune to obesity and eating disorders.

So, what exactly is this famine experience for kids? Kids can experience three basic types of famines:
1. delayed eating famines
2. quantity famines
3. quality famines.

Delayed eating famines

In the most common type of famine, kids run out of fuel before there is any more food available for them to eat. Many children tolerate "delayed eating" well and don't develop problems. But the vulnerable ones—and it is rather tricky to pick them out *before* they develop problems—often suffer terribly from the patterns that develop from this type of reckless eating behavior. By the time we notice their struggle and face the fact that it's not going to go away by itself, they may be trapped into years of eating struggles, endless diets, obesity, and all the turmoil these chronic problems bring.

This concept is extremely important to understand in order to help prevent kids from developing weight and eating problems. Remember, "delayed eating" doesn't refer to the time of day eating occurs. "Delayed eating" indicates a delay in time between when kids first feel hunger and the time when they actually eat food.

Delayed eating is usually involuntary, beyond kids' control. Many times kids must wait for lunch hour at school when they were ready for a meal at mid morning. Almost all kids report that they could easily eat lunch earlier than it is served. And many would take advantage of a mid-morning snack break if it were offered.

But delayed eating might be voluntary. For example, Tim is an overweight fifteen-year-old who tries to control his food intake by waiting until after school to eat a meal. He is convinced that avoiding food for the first half of his day will help him lose weight.

Delayed eating might also be unconscious. Kids may not be aware of their hunger. Particularly focused children tend to eat late unconsciously. They don't even realize they are hungry because their bodies' fuel-need signals don't get through their intense interest in something.

You may say, "Everybody has to wait to eat sometimes. People can't just eat anytime, anywhere, whenever they feel the first tinge of hunger." You are right. So how long does eating have to be delayed to trigger symptoms? That depends on several factors. Probably the most important is whether or not the child is physically active when hunger strikes. Even a delay of fifteen minutes for a hungry child who is playing hard can be significant. (More about this in Chapter 6.)

But hungry kids at rest are vulnerable if eating is delayed for thirty minutes or more. Individual kids vary widely in how well they tolerate delayed eating, and it's impossible to predict which ones will be affected in the long run. **So, it is always wise to minimize delayed eating with every child and teen.** Shoot for the ideal, which I call "eating on time." This is so important that it will be discussed in a separate section coming up.

Chronic delayed eating causes children and teens to lose touch with their natural eating instincts. Their appetites may surge to allow them to do make-up eating. Their fuel-need signals and fuel-full signals become unclear. Their taste for quality, healthful foods is replaced by preferences for low-quality, high-fat, high-sugar foods—often processed foods low in nutrients but high in concentrated calories.

These changes are actually adaptive but ultimately lead to unhealthy consequences. When children undereat and eat poor-quality foods intermittently over long periods of time (months), their eating will likely fall into a pattern that I call the Feast or Famine Cycle. This cycle explains how kids who don't eat well regularly develop adaptive eating patterns that may eventually lead to weight and/or eating struggles. But first let's talk about the two other types of famine: quantity and food quality.

Quantity famines

Quantity famines happen whenever kids don't eat enough food to meet their energy, growth, and metabolic needs. Many children and teenagers undereat for breakfast because they're rushing off to school and not feeling hungry when they first wake up in the morning. Then, when they do get hungry, they are in class and food isn't available. For these kids, and there are multitudes of them, the wait for lunch is long and uncomfortable. Their concentration in class also suffers without adequate fuel. *Missing or undereating breakfast is probably the most common type of quantity famine kids experience.*

Eight-year-old Tony, who plays on a little league team, gets terribly nervous when he has a game. He usually picks at his food on these nights although his parents encourage him to eat "for batting power." What can parents do in this situation? Isn't this a famine? Yes, it is, and it is unavoidable. Kids under stress can temporarily lose their appetites, and parents probably won't be able to override this natural inclination.

Occasional quantity famines—longer ones occuring during sickness—are inevitable and can be ignored. Some make-up eating may follow and that's OK. It's important for parents to learn to trust their kids' bodies while doing their best to keep good food available.

For example, fifteen-year-old Cheryl participates in dance line at her high school and practices right after school four afternoons a week. She eats first lunch at school at 11:50 and school is out at 3:15. Halfway through her rigorous practices Cheryl feels tired and famished. She has not eaten enough food at lunchtime to carry her through her practice.

Often kids simply can't eat enough food to take them through hours of vigorous exercise. The only way to prevent quantity famines from happening is to make more food available more often. Cheryl's mother's solution? Reminding her to pack a granola bar or sandwich to eat after school or during her break at dance practice.

Quality famines

Yes, food quality does count! Bodies are designed to use both calories and specific nutrients from food for energy, maintenance, growth, repair, and defense against disease. Calories are units of energy that kids' bodies use for all these functions, and calories are important to be sure. Inadequate caloric intake causes quantity famines, which we have just discussed.

Children and teens may get enough calories (units of useable energy) but not enough nutrients. This happens when kids regularly eat foods that are poor quality—typically higher in sugar and/or fat and low in nutrients. I call these foods "low-quality" foods because they offer the basic hunger satisfaction but don't nourish bodies very well. Favorite low-quality foods kids love include cookies, chips, soda pop, candy, donuts, ice cream treats, cake, and brownies. You can probably make your own list.

Quality famines usually stem from bad habits and lack of knowledge on the part of kids' caregivers. *Kids will eat the food they find around.* Children and teens can be very demanding and manipulative. They often coerce their parents into supplying lower quality (but tasty!) foods at home, where their availability becomes a chronic problem. These poor-quality foods are often very convenient, requiring no preparation. Kids typically prefer them to higher-quality foods that don't come in a bag or wrapper so the kids fill up on these empty calories and don't have room for higher-quality foods.

Carol is concerned about her son Ben, eight, who shows no interest in eating supper when he has spent a day with his grandmother. Grandma enjoys giving Ben treats while they are together, often sharing ice cream, candy, chips, soda pop, and a few of Grandma's special chunky chip cookies—all in the same afternoon! There is simply no room for high-nutrient foods in Ben's little body by the time he gets home at 5:30.

Quality famines very often accompany delayed eating. Delayed eaters prefer foods that are richer, with more condensed calories. These foods are better for make-up eating following a famine, as we will see in the section coming up. Famines demand that kids' bodies prioritize extra calories, often at the expense of the nutrient value. Let's see why.

The Feast or Famine Cycle

The pattern of adapting to intermittent famines, the Feast or Famine Cycle, involves two distinct phases. As we look at adaptive responses to famines in this pattern we can discover important relationships that can throw kids' eating behavior off track. This cycle demonstrates ways in which going hungry contributes to weight gain and disturbed eating in famine-sensitive kids. Be alert to these symptoms before weight or eating problems develop too far. Here is the diagram of the cycle:

The Feast or Famine Cycle

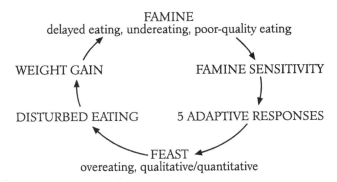

The two most obvious hallmarks of the Feast or Famine Cycle are:
- *triggers:* delayed eating, undereating, poor-quality eating (famines), and
- *symptoms:* overeating, qualitatively and/or quantitatively (feasts).

We will look at the famine phase of the cycle first because that's the starting point of all the adaptive responses (symptoms) that follow. The feasting is simply a result of delayed eating, undereating, and/or poor quality eating. And the feasting can take on several characteristics.

The famine phase of the Feast or Famine Cycle

The Feast or Famine Cycle always begins with a famine, or some type of undereating. All kids go hungry once in a while. This is unavoidable, and it usually lasts a relatively short time. But this is not the famine that starts the cycle. A true famine is a longer time when a child is hungry and consciously or unconsciously goes without food. Occasional famines are normal, but regular famines force kids' bodies to adapt.

Famines provoke the five adaptive responses I described in Chapter 1, to the degree that each individual child is biologically programmed to respond. Remember, the purpose of these biological responses is survival by storing extra fat.

The degree to which an individual child is affected by a famine—how strong these five adaptive responses are—depends very much on his or her *genetics*. All kids inherit specific traits or sensitivities from their parents, and the potential to adapt to famines is no exception. I use the term *famine sensitivity* to explain the differences in the ways kids' unique bodies respond to regular famines.

Some kids rarely suffer any cravings or excessive hunger, even though they go hungry at times, perhaps often. These kids are not very famine sensitive. They tend to be thin. Because they don't tolerate hunger well, they might be rather demanding when they get hungry. But, they may also be good at ignoring their hunger when they must and eating well when they get an opportunity.

Other kids don't fare as well with unsatisfied hunger. They may or may not tolerate hunger well, but their eating behavior is definitely affected by famines, sometimes dramatically. Following a famine experience or a series of regular famines, they experience powerful hunger pangs that demand bigger than normal meals. They also crave rich, sweet foods and think more about eating than others do. They may feel lazy and unmotivated after experiencing a famine and eventually feel tired in general.

These kids are very famine sensitive. They tend to gain weight easily and get a reputation for eating a lot. They never see going hungry or delayed eating as part of their problem. And their parents don't either. But it is. In fact, it's the trigger for all the struggles that follow.

Most kids are somewhere in between these two extremes. Moderate famine sensitivity means just that: Kids' bodies react to going hungry with moderate symptoms.

We'll discuss how to evaluate your child's famine sensitivity in Chapter 3.

The first thing to do to understand your child's vulnerability to weight or eating problems is to consider the role that ignoring hunger plays in triggering the Feast or Famine Cycle and the five adaptive responses. This will help you identify potential trouble spots as your kids move into different stages of growing up.

Once a pattern of undereating and/or poor-quality eating is established, kids with famine sensitivity will experience some degree of compensatory feasting. This allows their bodies to make up for lost calories in order to maintain their weight and ensure continued growth. The additional calories also provide excess fat for protection in future famines.

Kids' bodies that don't get enough fuel on a regular basis may store fuel (in the form of fat) to ensure survival through these feasting adaptations. Remember, individual bodies learn from the food supplied or lacking whether or not there is danger of famines in the future.

The feasting phase

Kids' bodies accomplish feasting by
1. taking in more calories
   a) eating more food
   b) eating calorie-condensed foods
2. conserving energy.

Several key adjustments happen in order for kids' bodies to take in more than the normal amount of calories. First, they become insensitive to their natural eating instincts, losing touch with their normal appetite signals and fuel-full signals. This allows them to overeat and do make-up eating following regular famine experiences. Second, they also conserve energy by lowering their overall metabolic rates and resisting physical activity.

Taking in more calories

1. *Kids lose touch with their hunger and fullness*

The most significant consequence of feast or famine eating patterns is that *kids lose touch with their natural appetite signals,* the ones they were born with. Undereating, delayed eating, and poor-quality eating force kids' bodies out of natural eating rhythms. Normal hunger is replaced by excessive hunger, and fuel-full signals become indistinct. So kids are more likely to overeat, both quantitatively and qualitatively. Children and adolescents who famine regularly often report that they are always hungry or never hungry. These are their bodies' adaptations to an insecure food supply.

It may appear that their bodies are defective and need more external dietary control, but this is not true. Kids who experience this loss of "body-controlled eating" inadvertently force their bodies to adapt to famines, creating a great danger of developing weight and eating problems that may last a lifetime.

Whether kids go hungry deliberately or accidentally makes no difference to their bodies' adaptive mechanisms. Going hungry simply requires a detachment from body signals that at one time kids were all perfectly in touch with. When children or teens lose touch with their immediate need for food, other natural fuel signals become indistinct in response. For example, in order to accommodate feasting (taking in excessive calories in make-up eating), kids must develop the ability to tolerate overeating. Overeating is normally an uncomfortable experience that kids naturally avoid by stopping when they feel full.

Eleven-year-old Tommy isn't hungry for breakfast and rarely eats even a piece of toast before school. Although he may be mildly hungry by noon, the school lunches are so unappealing that he eats little of the food on his tray. At five o'clock when his mother picks him up from the neighbor's, Tommy is so famished that he beelines it to the refrigerator.

Defying his mother's protests, he eats ice cream bars and leftover pizza. In spite of this binge-type snacking, Tommy eats the spaghetti dinner his mother prepares, with lots of garlic bread, as well as a brownie and ice cream dessert.

Rather than becoming a source of discomfort (standard equipment for all human beings), overeating feels comfortable and normal to kids who lose touch with their hunger signals. And as they tolerate both intense hunger signals and overfull signals, the Feast or Famine Cycle takes a firm hold. This is how kids get overweight and develop troubled eating behaviors.

2. Kids overeat (make-up eating)

The second and most obvious way for a body to catch up after inadequate food intake is to consume more food—*qualitatively and quantitatively.* Kids who overeat, binge, or do make-up eating not only eat more food, they tend to eat foods with more calories per bite. These richer, calorie-dense foods are the ones they crave when they have had to go hungry.

Madison, a nine-year-old, has fallen into the habit recently of eating an entire box of cookies as soon as she gets home from school. Her mother hides the cookies and puts fruit out on the counter in hopes that Madison will eat something healthier, but the little girl finds ice cream or the evening's dessert to eat instead. Upon questioning, Madison's mother finds that her daughter is not eating the school lunch because of a scheduling error that allows Madison only ten minutes in the lunchroom. Madison can hardly get through the line in that time. The real problem isn't Madison's bingeing on sweets. It's the daily famine she's experiencing at school.

Preoccupation with food is the setup for overeating, an important symptom to watch for in children. Talking often about eating, or an overemphasis on eating special, favorite treats, and the like, sometimes signal hidden famines in a kid's life. We'll discuss ways to check out these signals and what to do about them in the chapters to come.

Conserving calories

Besides increasing caloric intake through overeating, kids' bodies adapt to regular famines by burning less fuel in two ways:

- slowing metabolic rate
- avoiding physical activity.

Going hungry causes kids' metabolic rates to slow down. The more regular and more serious the famines are, the more significant this adaptive effect. Of course, genetic differences also play a role, but this adaptive response is universal. Kids who go hungry need to burn energy more slowly than kids who are eating plenty of great food regularly throughout the day. Unsure of the food supply, their bodies spend limited energy more sparingly.

Possibly as a result of this drop in metabolism, kids in famine mode experience physical depression. They adapt by avoiding physical activity. Again, the uncertain food supply causes these bodies to hold onto their fuel and spend it sparingly.

Many parents, physicians, and therapists believe that underactivity is the fundamental problem in overweight kids. Without looking at kids' terrible eating patterns, these parents try to get these kids moving more. But they are defeated before they begin. It's a dead-end road. The avoidance of physical activity in the famining child is only an adaptive symptom. To treat the symptom, rather than its cause, makes as much sense as giving oxygen to a person having difficulty breathing because his necktie is too tight.

Although the reluctance to be active in kids who experience famine is not psychological, a true depression can occur in kids who often go hungry. Lack of motivation, negative attitude, avoidance of challenge, moodiness, and many other manifestations of depression may be seen in kids suffering this effect. Probably a significant number of kids on antidepressant drugs are being treated for symptoms that could be relieved or at least improved by adjusting their food availability and eating schedules.

Is your kid on the Feast or Famine Cycle?

Look for these symptoms:
- regular overeating and/or bingeing
- preoccupation with food or eating
- frequent requests/preferences for sweets or high-fat foods
- eating from boredom, restlessness, especially at night
- eating in response to emotional upset or stress
- significant overeating on special occasions
- worries about appetite or eating behavior
- excessive hunger or symptoms of low blood sugar (headache, faintness, irritability, anxiety, confusion, feeling desperate when hungry).

Maybe you've noticed these symptoms before but didn't know what to make of them. Now you do. You're learning what to do about them and there's much more to come. If your kids don't have any of these symptoms, thank heaven for that, and know that you can learn how to protect them from the nightmare that this adaptive cycle brings.

Some kids seem to have much more trouble with eating and going hungry than others. Why do kids respond to varying food supplies so differently? Why do some kids seem so vulnerable to this Feast or Famine Cycle while others are evidently beyond its cruel effects?

GENETIC DIFFERENCES IN KIDS

3

Parents can prevent problems by assessing their kids' vulnerability to obesity and eating disturbances.

Every individual kid is unique. It is foolish, even dangerous, to ignore this important fact, especially regarding nutritional needs. Sure, there are patterns in development, patterns in eating behavior, and general principles of growth, personality, and socialization. But we will focus on the physical and physiological uniqueness of kids in this chapter. These areas of individuality are functions of kids' genetic blueprint, the purely inherited aspect of their bodies.

What can we do about that? Aren't genes unchangeable facts? You get the ones you get, and you give your kid the ones he or she gets and that's that. Right? I'm not about to suggest that kids' genes can be changed or that we would even want to do that. But we will look at the inherited genes that make kids more or less susceptible to unhealthy eating patterns. There are specific genetic predispositions to weight and eating struggles, and if you know about them, you, as care-givers, can do a lot to help a kid with these predispositions.

Famine sensitivity

All human beings have some degree of famine sensitivity. All bodies will adapt in various ways to famine. Many studies have been done concerning the effect of undereating (calorie restriction) on bodies, both normal and overweight. Our universal responses to this stress show that this is a fundamental adaptation—one that is linked to our basic survival as individuals and as a species.

But I have observed that individuals vary in their *degree* of famine sensitivity. This is true of kids as well as adults. All kids are famine sensitive to some degree. Calculating the degree of sensitivity is extremely helpful in preventing weight and eating problems. Let me explain how.

Famine sensitivity determines, more than anything else, an individual body's response to famines. For example, let's say two kids get lost in the woods for twenty-four hours with a canteen of water but no food. Both kids' bodies will adapt to this stress, but the degree to which this adaptation occurs will be unique for each kid. Notice the five adaptive responses to famine in these kids:

Reggie, who is ten years old, and his friend Adam, twelve, both begin to complain of feeling starved after a few hours (appetite increase), but Adam is the first to refuse to walk any farther (avoidance of physical activity). As the first day wears on, Reggie tells Adam he's getting cold (decreased metabolic rate) although the outside temperature is 75 degrees. As they begin to fall asleep, fifteen hours into their calamity, they talk about Thanksgiving dinner and their favorite foods (preoccupation with food), especially desserts (cravings for calorie-dense foods). Reggie declares that, as soon as he gets home, he's going to eat a whole batch of his mother's brownies (urge to overeat). Although each of these kids experiences the five adaptive famine responses, their bodies react uniquely based on their genetic differences.

High famine sensitivity

Although all kids are famine sensitive to some degree, some kids, just as adults, are much more famine sensitive than others. This is biological—inherited—and although you can't change it, you can cooperate with it to help ensure fewer weight and eating troubles. Kids who are highly sensitive to the famine experience have strong biological reactions to going hungry. The five adaptations in these kids are stronger than for those with average or low famine sensitivity. It is crucial for parents and caregivers to identify these kids in order to make a consistent effort to prevent famines from occurring. The rewards are well worth the extra effort.

So how do you identify kids with higher than normal famine sensitivity? Look first at their bodies. Are they overweight? If you are unsure, check with a doctor. Some kids are big and more dense than their peers, but they are not carrying too much fat. Next, look at the kid's gene pool—parents and close relatives—to find famine sensitivity in the family of origin.

Obesity and eating problems are not inherited directly, but the propensity for developing these troubles is definitely genetic. The factor that I consider paramount to this predisposition is famine sensitivity. High famine sensitivity in adults looks like this:

- weight problems
- eating struggles
- long and colorful diet histories
- wide weight fluctuations
- preoccupation with diets and body size.

For example, Janeen has a perfect little body at age three and a half. A body-controlled eater, so far she eats decent food most of the time. But Janeen's mother, Pat, has been dieting off and on since she was fifteen and is fifty pounds overweight. Pat's sister, not as heavy as Pat, is a dieter, too.

Janeen's dad is very tall, 6'4", but he is almost eighty pounds overweight and constantly trying to lose weight. His sister has never been heavy. Janeen's brothers, ages five and six, are normal weight.

Little Janeen shows no sign of weight or eating problems so far, but does her family tree indicate the likelihood that she will have problems in the future? Yes! Janeen's famine sensitivity is high, based on her parents' problems with weight. It is the genetics of the child's biological *parents*, more than anything else, that determines what that kid's level of famine sensitivity will be. Biological aunts, uncles, and grandparents may also point to a higher famine sensitivity, but parents are the best indicators. And when both parents have significant weight problems, they need to gear up to help that kid stay off the Feast or Famine Cycle. Remember, these kids don't need to learn to eat less food. They need to learn to never, ever go hungry and to eat only the best quality food as much as possible.

I have also observed that certain nationalities or ethnic groups have higher famine sensitivity in general. These include African Americans (especially women), Native Americans, and people of Spanish descent from Mexico. There must be something about the development of these people groups over the centuries that caused particularly high famine sensitivity to evolve as a necessary survival aid.

Low famine sensitivity

On the other end of the scale, some kids have low famine sensitivity. These kids' bodies don't react as strongly to the famine experience. They tend to tolerate famines without strong adaptive changes in appetite, metabolism, cravings, preoccupations and activity levels. In a way, their bodies are more resilient than those with higher famine sensitivity, and they don't generally develop serious weight or eating problems. But there are exceptions. The most common one is anorexia. Kids who tolerate going hungry and don't experience strong rebound appetite increases and weight gain may be more prone to chronic undereating as a lifestyle.

Moderate famine sensitivity

Obviously, most kids fall somewhere in this range—the norm. The amazing consistency in how kids' bodies respond to going hungry makes it possible to describe the common adaptive symptoms to famines. It is also very important to note that *throughout their development kids may vary from time to time in their own individual famine sensitivity.* In other words, a three-year-old child with one overweight parent may have moderate famine sensitivity. In early childhood he may react moderately to going hungry or develop poor-quality eating habits. But at puberty he may shift to higher famine sensitivity, reacting very strongly to going hungry. So, although we can estimate kids' famine sensitivity by looking at close relatives, all kids, themselves, will demonstrate their own unique famine sensitivity throughout their lives.

What's a parent to do?

Now that we know about this inherited piece, what can we do about it? Since all kids have some degree of famine sensitivity, *the ideal is to feed all kids only high-quality foods on time as much as possible.* Avoiding the Feast or Famine Cycle with its five symptoms of adaptation is the goal of every parent and caregiver, no matter whether a kid is especially vulnerable or not.

But, what special steps can parents take to keep kids with higher famine sensitivity out of danger? They can feed these kids well—extremely well—just as they would if the kids were diabetic. Why wait until they develop a serious metabolic disorder such as obesity?

Kids with higher sensitivity to all types of famines— eating recklessly, undereating and poor-quality eating—need help to keep their more sensitive bodies well fed at all times. This may require a big effort and considerable planning on the part of the adults in their lives. But the risk of weight gain and eating problems for life is so big, and these kids are so vulnerable, that it is worthwhile. Great effort on the front end can prevent enormous troubles for which there are few viable answers.

Feeding kids with high famine sensitivity

Remember, our central goal is to prevent kids with high famine sensitivity from experiencing famines by keeping them well fed on great food whenever they get hungry. This means *quantity famines* and *quality famines* must be avoided as much as possible.

So, good quality food must be made available *whenever* and *wherever* these kids get hungry. (These are the same basic goals for feeding all kids.)

Naturally, it's impossible to do this perfectly, but by consistently checking into our child's or adolescent's day-to-day life and troubleshooting food-need areas, we can identify and solve many problems before an eating or weight problem develops. For kids with high famine sensitivity, this is crucial.

Bob and Pam are both overweight and have struggled for years with diet and exercise. They have one five-year-old daughter, Lauren, and her weight is normal. Lauren is in kindergarten half days in the morning. She has cereal or French toast and fruit juice most mornings before school. There is a snack time at school at mid morning, and she brings her snack from home. Lauren's dad picks her up from school at noon and drops her at day care, where she has lunch—whatever is served. When her mom picks her up at 5:30, Lauren often complains that she is hungry and begs her mother to stop on the way home to get a treat. She continues to nag as her mother gets a quick dinner on the table, which Lauren eats with a frenzy. Before bed, Lauren often requests sundaes and cookies.

Both Bob and Pam are concerned by Lauren's behavior after day care. They're worried that she is going to develop a weight problem because of her focus on treats and demands for fattening foods at night. They don't want Lauren to experience the rejection and frustration of being a fat child but fear that her appetite is propelling her in that direction.

Troubleshooting Lauren's quality food availability

On the surface, Lauren's eating pattern doesn't look too bad, but a closer look reveals symptoms of the Feast or Famine Cycle. Lauren's hunger at the end of the day is excessive and it is specifically aimed at treats—condensed lower quality calories. It appears as if she is beginning to do make-up eating before bed as a result of some daytime undereating. Let's get more information to find out what the trouble spots are.

1. Is Lauren eating enough breakfast? Is the food substantial? Good quality?
2. What is Lauren eating for a school snack? Is it enough food to satisfy her hunger?
3. What is Lauren eating for lunch? Is it enough?
4. Is food available between lunch and 5:30?
5. What is Lauren eating between 5:30 and suppertime?
6. What is she eating for supper?

The answers to these questions are very revealing.

1. For breakfast Lauren is eating sugar-sweetened corn flakes with skim milk or French toast with butter and syrup. She drinks a small glass of fruit juice each day. Lauren appears to eat enough food at breakfast, usually everything in her bowl or on her plate.
2. Lauren's school snack is usually pretzels (her

mother knows these are low fat) or an apple.

3. The day-care facility provides lunch. A typical meal includes a pasta dish or casserole with vegetables, carrot sticks, milk, and jello or an ice cream bar for dessert. According to the day-care provider, Lauren always eats well at lunch, asking for second helpings occasionally.

4. Between lunch and 5:30 when her mother comes for her, Lauren gets busy playing with her favorite toys. Although a snack is offered at about 3:00, Lauren seldom notices. She seems perfectly content, according to the day-care provider.

5. Lauren's mother, Pam, tries to make her wait until they get home for a snack, but occasionally she'll run through McDonald's for ice cream cones, or she'll grab a candy bar at the gas station. Pam is starving, too, so it's hard to ignore her daughter's determined pleas.

6. Supper usually consists of SpagettiOs, macaroni and cheese, hot dogs, or hamburgers. Pam is not into cooking, and she is so hungry herself that it's too hard to be creative at this point in the day. Lauren's dad doesn't get home until after 7:00.

Recommendations for Lauren's parents

First, try to identify any quantity or quality famines in Lauren's school day. (Days with different schedules have to be assessed separately.) Lauren's breakfast consists of poor-quality food because of the high sugar content of sugarcoated cereals and the French toast is processed (pre-prepared and frozen). The syrup is almost entirely sugar.

Second, change to an unsweetened cereal. Lauren may use sugar on her cereal. She will likely use less than the presweetened cereal contains. The milk is good food, but skim milk is not appropriate for young children because their need for dietary fat is greater. Also the extra calories in 2 percent milk can help Lauren get to snack time more comfortably. If processed waffles, French toast, or pancakes are served, try using jelly or jam that is 100 percent fruit. Syrup is also OK if the food is not drowning in it.

Could Lauren eat more, or eat more substantial food at breakfast? Perhaps. This is a crucial question because some kids do better with heavier food first thing in the morning. Eggs, ham, pizza, bacon, and macaroni and cheese are some richer foods that kids might like, and even prefer, sometimes. And some kids, if they had the time, could easily eat two bowls of cereal instead of one. This is worth checking out and adjusting the morning schedule if necessary.

When kids become hungry mid morning, especially if they haven't eaten adequately for breakfast, light snacks, such as pretzels, are not enough to keep them going until lunch. They often become overhungry by then. Lauren's pretzel snack (low fat) is an example of "diet projection" by her mother, common among weight-conscious parents who fear their kids will struggle as they have with weight issues. It is perfectly understandable, but it backfires, just the same. Pretzels are poor-quality food. Apples are far superior and may be a perfect mid-morning snack for a kid who has eaten well for breakfast. Fruits and vegetables, cheese and crackers, dry cereal, peanut butter sandwich halves—these all qualify as decent snack foods. Find out what Lauren likes, keep these snacks on hand and send them to day care with her.

The day-care lunch sounds fine, without going into specific ingredients. Even if it's not the greatest quality food, it will not make or break a kid's eating patterns as long as it's eaten on time. Parents should focus on the meals and snacks that go before and after it, as long as lunch is not extremely poor quality. If day-care meals are very poor (and there are government guidelines for these meals), then parents or guardians will have to discuss with the provider ways to improve quality. I have heard of day-care facilities where hot dogs were served three days out of five. This type of situation should be changed, but from what I've heard from parents, it is the exception rather than the rule.

The day-care provider's information about Lauren missing the afternoon snack is very significant, however. Lauren may or may not be hungry at snack time, but because she is often preoccupied with other things, she misses the snack. Parents can advise caregivers to interrupt their "spaced-out" kids specifically to offer them something to eat. Maybe the kids won't want it then, but the snack can be offered again later, say at 4 o'clock and again at 5 so the child doesn't become overhungry.

Another thing to check out: What is the snack offered? It's important that Lauren like the snack, or she probably won't eat it even if she is hungry.

The ride home is obviously difficult for both Lauren and her mother. It's understandable why Pam stops for poor-quality emergency snacks, but unfortunately they provide calories without many nutrients. Pam can head off this crisis by preparing for this time of day. She can carry in the car some healthy snacks such as granola bars, almonds, peanuts, or cheese-and-cracker packets. Fruit juice and bottled water can help, too.

Dinner is so tough when both parents work away from home. The last thing they want to do at the end of the day when they get home, tired and hungry themselves, is fix a nutritious dinner. But it's possible to do without cooking for an hour. Specifics of this challenging area of prevention are coming up in Chapter 6.

This may all sound daunting, and perhaps a bit extreme. And it is, in a way. Where we have often made the mistake of underfocusing on our kids' eating patterns, the recommendations here are definitely overfocusing on them. This necessary shift is bound to feel odd at first. Kids' eating patterns and food availability simply must become much more important, much higher on our adult priority list, if we are going to protect our children from the traps of obesity and eating struggles.

Feeding kids with moderate famine sensitivity

Kids having at least one parent with weight problems and eating struggles (parents who are sensitive to quantity or quality famines) need the same kind of intervention that Lauren got from her parents. Daily schedules and activities must be evaluated for quality food availability and problem areas addressed. These kids may not be as vulnerable as those with very high famine sensitivity, but they still need caring adults to protect them from the pitfalls of the Feast or Famine Cycle.

Twelve-year-old Tony started playing basketball during third period at school this year. He has moderate famine sensitivity and has rarely experienced symptoms of the Feast or Famine Cycle. But since his schedule changed this year, Tony complains that he's starving by lunchtime at 12:40, and he can hardly get enough food to eat then. He buys double cheeseburgers and fries after school and still eats supper at home. Tony's parents are starting to worry about his "binge-ing" because his dad started to put on weight in high school and has had a problem ever since. Tony looks like he has added some extra padding to his face and around his middle since the beginning of the school year. This doesn't make sense to his parents because, with his daily basketball activities, he is more active than he has been in the past.

Troubleshooting Tony's quality food availability

Although Tony is not concerned, his parents are. And they're confused. What's going on here? Is this simply the genetic predisposition Tony has inherited from his dad? Is his eating the problem or the symptom of an underlying problem? Let's investigate by asking a few important questions:

1. Is Tony eating breakfast? What and how much?
2. What time is third period? How long does it last?
3. Is the 12:40 school lunch time the only slot in which Tony can eat?
4. What is Tony eating for lunch? Is there enough food? Does he have time to eat enough?
5. Are the double cheeseburgers Tony's only options after school?

As it turns out, Tony is not eating breakfast. He gulps down a big glass of OJ on his way out the door. "Don't have time to eat," is his alibi.

His mother says he hasn't eaten a good breakfast since he got into junior high, but he only started after-school fast-food bingeing this year. Skipping breakfast for Tony hasn't provoked symptoms of the Feast or Famine Cycle up to this point because he is not highly famine sensitive, and his activity level was much lower before getting into basketball.

Kids with very high famine sensitivity who routinely skip breakfast would probably be showing weight and/or eating problems by the time they are twelve, especially if they are involved in a sport or other regular physical activity. The growing number of young fat athletes confuses parents and health-care professionals who see exercise as the main solution to obesity in kids.

Third period begins at 9:45 and lasts 45 minutes. Tony is already in a famine by 9:45 because by then a big glass of orange juice is all used up by the metabolic and activity needs of a twelve-year-old body. Forty-five minutes of intense physical activity turns a significant famine into a very serious famine. Tony's body must scramble to adapt to this stressful situation. The demand for fuel increases, and there is no fuel available.

This illustrates two important principles regarding kids' activity levels:

1. Famines are intensified by increased activity.
2. Adaptive responses correspondingly increase in kids that famine with high activity levels.

Tony is done with basketball at 10:30. Once he cools down, he is very hungry at the beginning of his next class, but he has more than two hours before he can eat lunch. It's hard to concentrate, he says, and sometimes he gets a headache because he is so hungry.

Tony's lunch period is the last one at school. The first lunch starts at 11:40 and the second at 12:10. Schedules can usually be changed to adjust to a different lunch period.

Tony is eating pizza at lunch most days, but sometimes he has sloppy joes or burritos. Although he eats as fast as he can, he is still hungry when he goes back to class.

He also has milk or grape juice and some kind of dessert bar. Tony doesn't like vegetables and always passes them up.

Tony could go home to eat after school, but he is hungry specifically for cheeseburgers and fries, which he can't get at home. The fast food sounds perfect to him and he finally feels full after he's done with this meal.

This is a great illustration of a kid caught in the Feast or Famine Cycle. Tony's parents focus on his overeating because they don't see his undereating. Tony's body is scrambling to recover from his daily severe famines, and he is suffering all kinds of discomfort without a clue about what's going on. There are a few simple solutions to Tony's dilemma.

Recommendations for Tony's parents

It is crucial for Tony to eat breakfast every day. His parents will probably have to take charge of this at first because it requires maturity and discipline that few kids at twelve possess. The best breakfasts for Tony are richer foods he likes that have plenty of calories. These foods include eggs, cheese, peanut butter, bacon, ham and any lunch or dinner foods as well.

Tony may not prefer heavy foods in the morning because he is used to eating so much at night. So he can start with cereals and toast, shifting to richer, high-nutrient foods as his appetite adapts to a famine-free environment. Simply adding a substantial breakfast may solve, or nearly solve, Tony's problem. But let's suppose it doesn't. What else can Tony and his parents do?

Tony may still need to take a snack to school for sometime before lunch, especially if his lunch period can't be scheduled earlier. If eating during school hours is prohibited, special permission can be obtained for medical reasons. Preventing obesity and eating disorders is a valid medical reason. An earlier lunch period may help Tony immensely, even after he starts eating well for breakfast. Although it's a hassle, this change can improve his concentration and participation in his classes.

Tony's exaggerated hunger and inability to satisfy it with normal amounts of food are the direct result of the daily famines he is experiencing—symptoms of the Feast or Famine Cycle. Once the famines are eliminated, his lunch should return to normal.

Tony's cravings for fatty, rich foods (cheeseburgers and fries) in his make-up eating are also symptoms of his famine experience. Although these are not great quality foods because of their relatively high fat content, they are serving Tony's heightened appetite fairly well.

Shouldn't he be eating better quality foods? Yes, on a daily basis. But as his appetite calms down as a result of eliminating the daily famines he's been in, these cravings, and the bingeing that goes with them, will certainly diminish. He may need some help from his parents in choosing better quality food once he is off the Feast or Famine Cycle, but once his appetite returns to normal, they won't struggle so much to get his cooperation.

Low famine sensitivity

Once again, there's no basic difference between the prevention strategies for kids with high or lower famine sensitivity. But the fact is, some kids are not as sensitive to reckless eating, undereating, or going hungry. Consequently they are not as vulnerable to the Feast or Famine Cycle. These kids are blessed with famine tolerance. They *seem* to be naturally immune to weight and eating struggles no matter what or when they eat. They may go hungry, eat recklessly, eat lousy food and never suffer the slightest symptom of the Feast or Famine Cycle—at least not during their childhood or adolescence. Their bodies seem born to take all the variations in the food supply and not give the slightest hint of trouble.

At seventeen, it seemed like Camille was involved in almost every activity and sport at her high school. Six days a week and sometimes seven, she raced around from class to gym, campus to field and back. Sometimes she missed breakfast and frequently other meals as well. She loved sweets, particularly chocolate. But none of this ever affected her appetite or eating. Camille just ate when she could fit it in— sometimes a large meal just before bed—and her body adjusted. She had always been thin and able to tolerate going hungry.

Unfortunately, these children and teens are in the minority, and if you have one, you probably know it by now. But, as I've mentioned before, famine sensitivity can change during a kid's life, so it's important to help these kids to maintain body-controlled eating and stay off the Feast or Famine Cycle too.

Kids' body types and the effects of adolescence

All kids inherit a basic body type from their biological parents. There are three main body-type categories (mesomorph, ectomorph and endomorph), but our bodies are often combinations of these. It's important to talk about body types so that parents and caregivers can better appreciate their kid's unique size and shape. They can then be realistic in the way they view their kid's physique. Although we can make some generalizations about kids who fall into each of these three categories, there are always exceptions. We'll also explore how adolescence affects kids' bodies according to their individual body types.

Mesomorphic kids

Meso refers to muscle and morph comes from the Greek word for form. Kids with this body type are generally muscular and tend to move around a lot from the time they are born. These kids are often athletic and/or physical in their play preferences. They tend to be well-proportioned. They are stronger than peers who have different body types, and they often weigh more than less muscular friends. Because of their relatively higher percentage of muscle and a tendency for higher activity, mesomorphic kids tend to burn calories faster and get hungry more often. Because of these factors, they may actually be more prone to the Feast or Famine trap.

Before puberty, mesomorphic girls and boys look similar. These are not the petite kids on the block, although they may not be tall for their age. Their bodies are strong and muscular and solid. Once puberty hits, clear distinctions emerge between the sexes, but the basic mesomorphic structure remains.

At puberty, the female hormone that most influences body-shape changes in all girls is estrogen. Its most visible effect is to add fat in strategic locations: breasts, hips, and thighs. Between ages eleven and fifteen girls usually add some padding that softens their angular build. As long as mesomorphic girls remain body-controlled eaters, this weight and fat accumulation will be perfect for their development, and they will continue to enjoy their more muscular bodies in sports and other physical activities.

But some girls, prone to interfering with their natural eating instincts during this time, begin to diet or simply start going hungry because of busy schedules and poor planning. This triggers the Feast or Famine Cycle and its adaptive responses. The symptoms of the Cycle—increased appetite, lowered metabolic rate, cravings for sweets and fats, preoccupation with food, and activity avoidance—sometimes cause genuine panic in these adolescents.

At fourteen, Liz had always been the smallest girl on her cheerleading team. Although very strong and muscular, she was so short (5'1") that she was the perfect person for the team to toss into the air for their routine grand finale. When she gained a little weight before her sophomore year in high school, she had no idea what this would do to her position on the team. The team captain informed Liz that she would be replaced by a different girl—taller but thinner. The news devastated Liz and she began to diet strenuously.

This eating pattern, coupled with her athletic lifestyle, put her on the Feast or Famine Cycle and eventually led her into bulimia. She simply didn't have enough confidence in her body during this period of growth and change to resist interfering with her normal weight gain. Unfortunately, *many* adolescent girls don't.

Mesomorphic boys are the envy of boys with other body types. Natural built-in muscle supports a boy's identity as strong and masculine. These boys often comprise the athletic teams during childhood and adolescence. Because the male hormone testosterone is responsible for increasing muscle development in all boys, regardless of body type, boys in general don't experience the fat deposition influence of estrogen that girls do. Instead, all boys develop bigger, stronger muscles, even if they are not particularly active or athletic. Of course, the mesomorphs who are involved in sports gain the most muscle of the three groups.

Are mesomorphic boys vulnerable to the Feast or Famine Cycle during adolescence? The ones with high famine sensitivity are, but there is a built-in inhibition to the effects of the Cycle. Here's why: Boys under the influence of the muscle-building hormone testosterone who are already prone to be muscular, usually have trouble keeping up with their bodies' need for calories. Consequently they display very big appetites in general. When they eat, they eat big. Although they grow—and intermittently they grow at high speed—they probably don't regularly eat enough extra calories for additional fat accumulation. In other words, they may cycle but their make-up eating usually isn't enough to overshoot their heightened metabolic and growth needs. Muscle tissue uses more energy to maintain as well, so these boys often race to get enough food in to keep their growing, muscular bodies fueled.

Because of this high fuel demand during adolescence, mesomorphic boys need to be eating plenty of good food whenever they get hungry. Their school performance, good judgment, mood, self-control, athletic performance—every aspect of life—will improve when they do.

Mike was a classic mesomorph, wrestling in the lightweight category for his high school. At 98 pounds, he was all muscle and a very talented athlete, even as a freshman. His coach, who wanted to keep him in the lightweight category, let Mike know that he expected him to keep his weight down for matches and tournaments. Otherwise Mike wouldn't qualify to compete.

So, like many of his teammates in the same situation, Mike did what he had to do: He fasted, he soaked in hot water to sweat his weight down, he spit into a towel during the days of the meets. Mike made weight every meet because he was so determined. But it cost him. He lost several important matches simply because he was too weak. After wrestling season he began to gain weight—not muscle weight, but flab around his middle. Mike's fasting and dehydrating strategies put him on the Feast or Famine Cycle, but he didn't have a clue what was happening to his body. Fortunately, he gained enough weight naturally during the summer to force him into the next weight category for his sophomore year.

Ectomorphic kids

This body type is slender and can be the most worrisome for parents during their kids' childhoods. (Ecto means outside.) Kids with ectomorphic builds are naturally very slim and may also have correspondingly slight appetites. While many parents are watching for signs of overeating and weight problems in their children, the parents of these beanpoles are trying to get them to eat more and gain weight!

Ectomorphs may indeed appear to be too lean, but they are almost always just right for their natural body type. They are lighter than their more muscular peers and actually require fewer calories to maintain their energy and growth. They tend to pay little attention to eating and may forget to eat because they are engaged in an activity they enjoy.

Is it important for ectomorphic kids to eat well and stay off the Feast or Famine Cycle? You bet it is. Even though these kids usually do not gain weight easily, the stresses of going hungry and adapting to poor food availability are not good for any kids. They'll suffer whether or not their bodies actually show outward signs of their distress.

Tall and lean himself, Bill is father of a fifteen-year-old boy, and a girl, just turning thirteen. "I wish I could get them to gain weight, he confides. They're both so skinny, even though their mother is on the heavy side. My son is a football player and I'm concerned he'll get hurt because some of the other boys on the team are so much heavier. Nothing works, though. He's tried a dozen different ways to gain weight. My daughter? She loves being so thin. She's 5-8 and wears a size zero!"

When ectomorphs, both boys and girls, hit puberty, they tend to stay slim. The curves ectomorphic girls and boys develop are more subtle. Both groups may complain because puberty doesn't show much on the shape of their bodies, and they may feel they don't fit in with their curvier peers. While the girls would like breasts that show, the boys complain of being too skinny and not manly enough. These kids may need support for their angular looks, but sometimes they are perfectly happy with their skinniness, especially the girls. Whatever the case, ectomorphic kids need to learn to remain body-controlled eaters so they can enjoy their natural leanness permanently.

Endomorphic Kids

The endomorphic category is a fat body type. *Endo* is Latin for inside. Are kids born fat? Well, to tell the truth, some are. I've seen some newborns weighing in at ten pounds who were visibly very fat. But that's not what this category is about. Usually kids' body types emerge after a year or so, once they're up and walking a bit. Before this, all babies actually need extra fat for metabolic emergencies, sickness, and those inevitable falls. So babies have some obvious extra fat. It's one of the things that makes them so cute.

Some kids inherit an endomorphic body type that seems to make them prone to obesity. Perhaps these are the bodies that tend to be more highly famine sensitive. Endomorphic kids tend to carry their weight in their midsection, and their limbs tend to be relatively normal-sized. This feature may only become obvious after age three because many children younger than this who are not endomorphs also have relatively bigger middles. In fact, as long as these kids stay slim, endomorphic kids look pretty much like everybody else. It's only when they begin to put on weight that endomorphs look like endomorphs. This is because the extra weight tends to go to one place—the midsection.

There seems to be a predominance of endomorphism in certain ethnic groups. The strong propensity of kids from these subgroups points to the genetic influence. These groups include African Americans (those that have been in America for generations), Native Americans, and Mexicans.

Endomorphic kids often enjoy fairly normal bodies during childhood, but not always. Those who do, usually experience a bumpy road when puberty strikes.

With a Native-American grandmother and Mexican father, Rachel had a lovely tawny complexion and pitch-black hair. During grade school, she was always one of the shortest girls in her class. and she enjoyed a petite figure. Around her tenth birthday, though, Rachel began to develop breasts and put on weight around her middle. By the time she went to high school four years later, Rachel was obviously overweight. She especially looked fat because most of her extra weight hung around her waistline.

Girls with this body type sometimes gain weight dramatically under the influence of estrogen and may find themselves in a totally different body between the ages of eleven and fourteen. With this dramatic weight gain (which may be the result of reckless eating, famines, and diet attempts), many girls start to diet consciously, and many more unconsciously try to control their food intake. Almost all kids, boys and girls alike, have busy schedules that interfere with their eating, whether or not they are trying to lose weight. Whatever the cause, the result is the same: Feast or Famine Cycling in kids who tend to gain weight very easily.

Endomorphic kids do not need to try to become athletes like mesomorphs, and they will never look like their friends who are ectomorphs. Kids with this body type need the careful support of their caregivers to keep them off the Feast or Famine Cycle by ensuring that they avoid quantity and/or quality famines as much as possible. Endomorphic kids don't need less food and more exercise. They need plenty of quality food, possibly more often than other kids. This is the only way to avoid weight and eating problems and give these vulnerable kids a chance for a normal body and life.

Growth spurts

One of the things that can dramatically affect appetite in kids is their erratic periods of accelerated growth. Sometimes kids go through these times with extra hunger—hunger that can be alarming to parents who are not clued in to their kids' body signals.

But kids' bodies, left to their natural instincts and supplied with great quality food, will get what they need—no more, no less. In fact, it's important to be sure to keep up with these intensified appetites. Boys and girls who are in growth spurt periods are more vulnerable to famines because their caloric needs are heightened.

On the other hand, following this surge, kids' appetites can become suddenly lower, and this, too, can cause parents' concern. Just remember, kids' bodies know what they're doing. Keep focused on what you're supposed to be doing: making good quality food available for your kids to eat whenever they get hungry. As long as you stick to your job, your kids' bodies will do just fine.

Part Two:

How Can We Teach Kids Good Eating Behavior?

BODY- CONTROLLED EATING

4

Help your kids stay tuned in to their bodies.

In order for kids to avoid the Feast or Famine Cycle and all the eating and potential weight struggles it brings, they must stay attuned to their natural eating instincts and remain "body-controlled" in their eating.

Body-controlled eating means that kids trust their bodies' fuel need signals by

1. eating on time and avoiding going hungry as much as possible
2. eating only high-quality food when hunger strikes.

This may sound like a fairly simple formula for such a great reward as natural lifelong eating freedom and weight control, but in our culture it is very challenging to implement. The difficulties mainly lie in the busyness of our lifestyles and the hang-ups we have about weight and eating behavior.

Children and teens who avoid weight and eating problems tend to have natural lower famine sensitivity and keep their bodies in charge of their food needs, relying on their bodies' signals for eating behavior. They use their intellects (and those of their caregivers) only for anticipating their hunger (preparing for fuel needs in advance so food will be available) and choosing quality foods.

These kids don't fall prey to the misleading messages of our diet-crazed culture (e. g., you can never be too thin, you must carefully control your diet or you will be fat, looks are everything). And they usually have parents who support their body-led eating behavior. They remain body-controlled in their eating, for the most part, as they were when they were born. Consequently they avoid the quagmire of the Feast or Famine Cycle.

As caregivers of kids, we are entrusted with the tasks of teaching and reminding kids of the simple principles of body-controlled eating, and helping our kids by providing good food whenever it is needed. So first we must know what these principles are.

Principles of body-controlled eating for kids

1. Hunger is always a legitimate signal that food/fuel is needed. Satisfy it with quality food as soon as reasonably possible.
2. Make good-quality food—meals or snacks— available at regular intervals (at least every three hours or so—and continuously for kids under five).
3. Do not make poor-quality (low-nutrient) foods regularly available.
4. Internal cues (fuel-full or satisfaction signals) are the only valid cues to stop eating.
5. Whenever possible, ignore external cues (time of day, others eating, time limitations) and intellectual cues (I should not eat now because I just ate an hour ago) to eat or stop eating. Allow the body to govern eating behavior.

6. When making food choices, take into account cravings, aversions, and interest in various types of foods.

Principle #1:
Hunger is always a legitimate signal that food/fuel is needed. Satisfy it with quality food as soon as is reasonably possible.

Eating on time

First and foremost, kids must eat on time—very soon after the time they get hungry—as much as possible. Natural eating occurs in response to hunger because hunger is the signal that fuel is running low and the body needs calories and nutrients. *Whether or not a child usually eats on time has much more to do with his/her weight and eating behavior than has ever before been acknowledged.* The reason is simple: Bodies are designed to take in food most efficiently soon after perceiving hunger. And as we have seen in the Feast or Famine Cycle adaptations, bodies will make physiological adjustments when food is not eaten at these times.

Eating on time is the opposite of delayed eating. It has nothing to do with the clock or dinner bell, although most naturally thin people (body-controlled eaters), eat at regular intervals and tend to get hungry at the times they routinely eat. With few exceptions, naturally thin people—adults and kids alike—have a strong tendency to eat on time consistently. They don't tolerate hunger well because it causes them discomfort. On the other hand, I have observed that kids with weight and eating problems often don't eat on time. They tend to eat late, regularly delaying meals for an hour or more. There are many reasons for this, but the most potent and universal culprits will be discussed later in this chapter under factors that interfere with body-controlled eating.

Kids may need to be reminded that they can and

should trust their hunger signals, particularly if they have a weight problem, real or imagined. Hunger is not psychological. It is physical. And kids need to understand that their hunger is a simple request by their bodies for food. If their natural eating patterns have not been confused by regular famines, diet misinformation, and/or interference by adult caregivers, this won't be too difficult.

But contradictory and confusing messages about hunger, food, and eating bombard kids growing up in our culture and threaten to infect them at any time. This is why caring adults must be aware and proactive in reinforcing healthful attitudes about hunger and eating.

Children of all ages are sometimes unaware of their own hunger because of overriding conditions such as fatigue, preoccupations, and intense physical activity.

For example, Troy, seventeen, comes home from a baseball game looking beat.

"How was the game?" his mom asks. "You look exhausted."

"I am exhausted. We lost," Troy says.

"Are you hungry?"

Troy pauses, thinking. "Thirsty for sure. Yeah, as a matter of fact I am hungry."

"I'll make stir fry. There's orange juice in the fridge," Mom says.

"Make a lot," Troy calls back as he leaves to shower. To reassure our kids that their bodies are always right about hunger, we may need to invite them to eat and remind them that it's OK to be hungry whenever that occurs. But don't badger them! Some need encouragement to admit that they're hungry, especially if they have a real or imagined weight problem.

Angela is only eleven, but she is self-conscious about her pubescent body and softening shape. She is beginning to ask about diets and talk about her friends who are dieting.

Her mother is aware of the danger of the eating avoidance trap, so she talks to Angela about how important it is to stay tuned in to her body signals in order to stay naturally thin and avoid unnecessary weight gain. Mom also leaves a note on the kitchen table with the reminder: Snacks in fridge.

Parents play a vital role in the process of teaching and reinforcing body-controlled eating. Modeling such behavior is at least as important as anything they say. More on this modeling role for parents in Chapter 8.

Unfortunately, we sometimes teach our kids to ignore their hunger and thirst both subtly and overtly:

"Oh, it won't hurt you to skip breakfast now and then. I never ate breakfast when I was a kid," one father teases his hungry, complaining ten-year-old.

"Going hungry is good for your character—a little pain never hurt anybody," a grandmother philosophizes as her grandson, seven, asks for a snack an hour before supper.

A day-care provider assures parents that there is absolutely no eating except at scheduled snack or mealtimes because "there are too many fat kids out there already."

"You can't just eat any time you get hungry," a frantic mother explains to her fussing four-year-old. "We had lunch and you should have finished your sandwich or else you wouldn't be hungry now. We'll eat dinner when we get home and maybe you will clean your plate then!"

As caregivers we must beware of our own poor thinking habits while we train children and teens in body-controlled eating behavior.

Body signals for food (as well as liquids, rest, sleep, and exercise) are always significant messages that should be heeded if possible. Kids need to be taught to pay attention to these need signals and never ignore them. It's easy for human beings of any age to be distracted by all the things going on outside the body so that physical need signals are ignored. But in order for bodies to run at top efficiency, it is important that their needs be met as much on demand as possible. The consequences of ignoring these all-important signals from our bodies are potentially very serious.

Principle #2:
Make good-quality food—meals and snacks—available at regular intervals (at least every three hours, and continuously for kids under five).

Principle #1 depends on this second principle, so they are both top priorities in body-controlled eating. As long as kids always eat when hunger strikes, the only decision kids must make when they get hungry is what to eat. And what they choose depends entirely on what foods are available. *Kids need to have good quality food available at very regular intervals.*

At first, this simple recommendation may sound unnecessary, even ridiculous. A conscientious parent may protest, "I already have food around for my kids. They can eat whenever they want, except snacking right before a meal. What's this 'make food available' all about?"

Although it seems to most parents and caregivers that kids have plenty of food to eat when they get hungry, often a little investigation reveals that this is not always so. Besides, the body-controlled eating principle reads "Make good quality foods—meals and snacks—available to kids at regular intervals, at least every three hours." This type of regular, quality food availability is different from simply having edible food around for kids to eat.

Unless all the food choices kids have are within the good/better/best category, quality famines will occur. Kids may get calories when needed, but because their nutritional status is still poor, they may develop symptoms of the Feast or Famine Cycle.

On the other hand, many adults think their kids are

eating whenever they get hungry, but they are not. Kids often suffer through periods of hunger daily (more painful and difficult for some kids than for others) and never think to mention it to Mom or Dad. The times that kids most frequently become overhungry because of a lack of availability of food are these:

- between breakfast and lunch, (particularly if they missed or underate at breakfast)
- after school or late afternoon (when activities, such as sports, interfere with eating).

Optimal food availability is easier to achieve once you understand how important it is. It is not necessary for kids to live in or near a pantry superstocked with nutritionally superior foods, ready to eat twenty-four hours a day. But the ready availability of decent (nutrient-rich) foods is crucial in order for kids to maintain body-controlled eating and avoid quality famines.

Regular meals, which are essential, consist of at least three substantial quantities of food eaten at intervals fairly evenly spaced during the day. *Substantial* is a relative term, based of course on the size and activity level of the kid. A quality toddler meal, for example, certainly wouldn't be substantial for a fourteen-year-old.

Snacks are relatively smaller portions of quality foods eaten between larger meals. We usually think of snacks in our country as sweets and munchies, such as candy bars and chips, but these lower quality foods are not appropriate for kids because they are so nutrient poor.

Stock plenty of good-quality food that kids like and that they can eat for meals or snacks whenever they get hungry. This includes foods that are ready to eat, such as fresh fruits, veggies with dip, unsweetened cereals with milk (sugar is OK as a condiment), breads and fillings for sandwiches, cheese and crackers. Soups can be prepared in minutes. Leftover foods from meals are great for between-meal snacks.

Juices of all kinds—100% juice—hold off anxious appetites well, close to mealtimes. You'll find more specific information on food in Chapter 5 and in the Appendix.

Principle #3:
Do not make poor-quality (low-nutrient) food regularly available to kids.

- Kids will eat the food they like that is available to them when they get hungry.
- Kids will not eat food that is not available.

This is a profound, if obvious, set of facts. Adults must pay attention to these two simple realities if kids are going to stay well-fed and avoid eating problems. The responsibility for kids' food quality rests squarely on the shoulders of their care-givers—those who bring food into the house.

- *Do not buy* food that you know is poor quality (very high-fat foods, high-sugar foods, highly processed foods).
- *Do not buy* food that you may have to argue with your kids about eating.
- *Do not bring* tempting food into your home that you know you yourself should not eat.

Does this mean that adults can completely prevent kids from having unhealthy foods ever? Of course not. Poor-quality foods surround us, and kids can get them without our help. *But we can make sure that only decent, healthful foods are easy to get in our kids' normal everyday environment.* Parents control the food in the home, day-care providers choose foods for the day-care center, school cafeterias stock school lunch food, and sometimes breakfast foods as well.

So how do we make good choices? Mary is a home-maker and mother of three children, ages seven, nine and fifteen. She usually does the grocery shopping for the family. But her husband, Mike, helps out occasionally. Mary set up strict rules about the foods she keeps in her house when she recovered from her own weight/eating problem after her last child was born. She has learned to limit her grocery list to only high-quality foods, so those are the only foods available to eat at home. Mary doesn't buy soda pop or chips of any kind. She doesn't buy pastries, ice cream, dessert foods, candy, or presweetened cereals. She doesn't bake sweets or desserts either.

So what do her kids eat for snacks? Mary buys all kinds of fruits and nuts, granola bars, and regular cereals that her kids like. She buys soups, bread, and peanut butter and jelly. And she buys cheese and crackers—a favorite snack at her house. This isn't Mary's complete list, but you get the point: When kids get hungry, they will eat the food they like that is available. They will not eat any food that is not available.

In my seminars on this topic, some worried mother always gets a frightened look on her face when admonished to make these changes in her grocery list. "But, you don't mean...well do you mean I can't bake cookies for my kids, or a birthday cake, for heaven's sake?"

I am always glad to reassure her that I never tell parents or day-care people, or anybody for that matter, what specific foods they should provide for kids. The question to answer is, "What is the overall quality of the foods that kids in my charge are getting day to day?"

You can probably improve it—perhaps dramatically. Just decide and then do it. You may get some flack when the chips and ice cream bars disappear, but hold on. Kids recover from the shock. And making these changes is so important for their future health. You're setting eating patterns for life here!

Principle #4:
Internal cues (fuel-full or satisfaction signals) are the only valid cues to stop eating.

Babies and little kids can't eat beyond their body signals, no matter what adults try to do to get them to eat more. They have a wonderful internal mechanism that makes them stop—sometimes right in the middle of a bite! Parents coax, play games, threaten, trick, and otherwise try in vain to shovel into their kids the amount of food adults think their kids need.

But kids' bodies rule! These little bodies know exactly what they're doing. This fact should be very reassuring to parents everywhere and it could help prevent the kinds of food abuses that have been happening to kids' bodies for eons. Parents can relax, knowing that they can trust their kids' fuel-full signals. It's OK to let them leave food uneaten on their plates and in their bowls. Even really skinny kids are rarely in physical danger from eating only the amount of food they want. They are usually just naturally skinny for that period of their childhood. The tricky part is making sure the food kids eat is good stuff. After that, let them eat the amount they want.

Remember the example, earlier in the book, of the baby spitting out the applesauce after several enthusiastic bites? I learned about this phenomenon from my first baby, Michael. I call it the "one bite threshold." It is a powerful example of the ability of kids' bodies to manage fuel intake and limits.

Kids all have excellent internal food-need cues along with their fuel-full signals. You can count on their bodies to know when they need to eat, and how much. If they're on the Feast or Famine Cycle, and have needed to adapt to famines, their fuel-need and fuel-full signals may have become somewhat distorted. But they can recover normal hunger and fullness signals as quality food becomes consistently available.

Unlike Mikey's one-bite threshold story, as kids get older, their parents may actually be able to force them to eat more food and more of certain types of foods, even when they protest that they are full. But this coercion can create three problems:

First, their bodies don't need the extra food we're forcing them to eat. Their bodies are not signaling for more food. Therefore, the food goes to waste in their bodies, just as if it were left on the plate. Only this is worse because the coercion has violated the body-controlled eating principles.

Second, forcing kids to eat when they are full is abusive and negatively affects the relationship between the parent/caregiver and the kid. As with any kind of abuse, coercion erodes trust.

Third, when they are forced to eat by their parents' ideas of what and how much they should eat, kids may learn to get their eating cues from outside their own bodies. They stop trusting their own body signals.

Principle #5:
Whenever possible, ignore external cues (time of day, others eating) and intellectual cues (I should not eat now because I just ate an hour ago) to decide whether or not to eat.

Research has shown that external cues motivate the eating behavior of obese adults more than non-obese adults. In other words, people with weight problems tend to tune in to eating prompts from the environment more often than from their own internal hunger sensations.

Dieters in general, I have observed, tend to eat according to what they think they should eat, the amount they think they should eat, and when they are allowed to eat. But people who enjoy natural leanness are almost always tuned into their internal body signals. This is why it is so important to teach kids to pay attention to their internal cues and ignore the external pressures to eat or not to eat, including their own self-talk.

Kim joined the drama club at her high school her freshman year. The club had play practice every morning before school at 6:20, and the school provided breakfast for them right after practice, before first hour. At first, Kim thought this breakfast at school would work out great. She wouldn't have to get up even earlier to eat before school. But it didn't work out at all because the first day of play practice, Kim suffered through the whole practice, starving and feeling weak. When she complained about it at home, Kim's mother helped her realize she simply couldn't wait until 7:15 to eat breakfast when she was getting up so early.

"But all the other kids are!" Kim protested.

"You're not all the other kids," her mother reminded her.

So Kim and her mother made sure she got up early enough to eat before practice and when the club went for the school breakfast, Kim went too. She ate again if she was hungry or just talked with her friends if she wasn't.

Kids don't usually look at the clock to see if they should eat. Body-controlled eating is always governed by internal cues just the way newborn babies demand feedings and stop eating based solely on their hunger and fullness. Any cue outside a kid's body signals should be ignored unless there is a practical and necessary reason to heed it.

Principle #6:
When making food choices, take into account cravings, aversions, and interest in various types of foods.

Within the vast array of food types available to us, we can find a lot of variety for our kids' food choices. Kids' appetites generally reflect their nutritional needs when they are offered a variety of healthful foods. Their bodies know what they need—the basic principle behind body-controlled eating. Therefore, when buying food, it is very important for parents to take their kids' taste preferences into account.

In one family, we can see this clearly. Little Ellen, age six, loves cantaloupe and apples and peanut butter toast. But her brother, Shawn, who is seven, hates cantaloupe and prefers bananas to apples. He used to like peanut butter (until he threw up a peanut butter and jelly sandwich), but lately he has become enamored with tuna salad and grape juice. Thank God, Peter, the baby, will eat anything!

Children and teenagers can be finicky eaters, but you can still encourage body-controlled eating in those kids. Simply work with those quality foods (however few they may be), and have faith that these kids' bodies will eventually shift, broadening their palate to include more variety. Keep offering a variety of foods and encourage (don't force) tasting different things.

In fact, finicky eating could have a biological basis. Research with babies has shown that, over several days, they choose a balanced diet with foods that contain nutrients they need. Although they may not choose a balanced meal each time they eat, their instinctive selections cover the spectrum of their fuel and nutrient needs every two or three days. We can safely assume that, for biological reasons, certain kids may tend to prefer some and shun other foods in more extreme ways from time to time. They always grow out of these phases, according to parents. But finicky eating can be a real source of frustration to adults trying to provide good meals to more people than just the finicky kid. Aside from the frustrations of trying to feed these resistant types, there is no danger to their health from their pickiness.

What body-controlled (natural eating) looks like in kids

Now that you're familiar with the six principles of body-controlled eating, let's look at some more examples that illustrate these principles.

Sophie and her sister, Lindsay, are two-year-old twins. They are fraternal twins so they do not share the same exact genetics that identical twins do. Actually, they are quite different from each other. Though they share the same hair and skin coloring, Sophie is taller and more active. She also weighs three pounds more than her sister, which is quite a lot on such small frames.

The more serious eater of the two girls, Sophie rarely misses a full meal or snack whenever she gets hungry, which is frequently earlier in the day. Sophie has one breakfast at home and then another at day care an hour later. Her sister, Lindsay, is more petite and delicate. Lindsay prefers to play quietly while her sister is romping around the yard with the older boys. Sid doesn't seem as interested in food during meal or snack times and often leaves something on her plate.

The twins' parents and day-care providers face a classic challenge. They must allow each of these two little girls to be in charge of her own eating, supporting their individual differences in timing, food type, and quantity. The parents accomplish this by following the six principles of body-controlled eating, paying attention to each individual girl, never comparing, and supporting their unique appetites and preferences

Isabella, almost nine, lives with her grandmother. This little girl seems interested in everything but eating. She "forgets" to eat breakfast sometimes because, she says, she just "isn't in the mood to eat." Isabella usually eats lunch at school, but the important thing about lunch is the social time, not the lunch.

Her grandmother keeps her favorite foods at home, and Isabella simply helps herself at any time of the day. Grandma says, "I hardly notice her eating. She just slips it in and never mentions it. Doesn't seem important to her, but she eats, that's for sure."

Luke, age fourteen, is playing football for his fifth season. He is tall for his age, 5'10", and very slim at 140 pounds. Luke never misses a meal because he gets ravenous between them. His parents noticed this about him even before adolescence. When she has time, Luke's mother fixes him a big breakfast (he is starving in the morning) and buys substantial foods he likes that he can fix himself for breakfast—including his favorite pizza. He's hungry again by after-school practice time so Luke's mom helps him plan for a meal out or packs a nutritious snack so he doesn't "get weak." Luke doesn't tolerate going hungry well, so he and his parents make eating on time a priority for him.

At eighteen, Gabrielle has settled into an eating pattern that works for her schedule and her body. Her mother has helped her plan for her meals during the day so she doesn't get stranded without decent food. Because she is in school and works part time as well, she has to prepare for the day with her hunger in mind. Gabrielle packs two lunches every weekday morning. She knows she'll need them before she gets back home after eight. Occasionally, she eats out, but this is expensive and often too time consuming for her schedule, so she tries to stick to meals from home.

Now that we know the basics of natural or body-controlled eating, and how it can work for various kids, let's recap some potential problem areas.

Factors that interfere with instinctive (body-controlled) eating

Since the most basic issues in body-controlled eating are eating on time and eating only high-quality foods, problem areas center on these two issues.

Reasons kids don't eat on time:

1. kids' schedules and caregivers' schedules
2. poor planning for food availability

3. focused personality (distracted from food needs)
4. conscious choice because of anxiety about weight (the kid and/or the adult)
5. high tolerance of hunger (low incentive)
6. adult prejudice or ignorance about normal eating.

Bear in mind that several factors may influence individual kids' eating habits, so they may experience famines often, though for various reasons. Chapter 5 deals entirely with these problem areas so you can troubleshoot your kids' individual vulnerabilities.

Reasons kids don't eat high-quality foods when they get hungry:

1. Caregivers don't make high quality foods accessible.
2. Tasty, convenient, poor-quality foods are readily accessible for kids.
3. Caregivers don't know the difference between great foods and lousy foods.
4. Adults or kids don't plan, or plan well, for kids' quality-food needs away from home.

We can all relate to these obstacles to optimal eating for our kids, but don't be discouraged. No matter where you are on the map now, there are definite directions to your goal to ensure your kids' healthy eating patterns in the future— for life!

Running Interference

5

Head off the factors that interfere with body-controlled eating.

We are a nation of human doings. Everybody always seems to be busy and our kids are no exception. Kids are running here and there with school, sports, music lessons, dance, 4-H, Girl Scouts, church activities, field trips, and their own social lives, not to mention family time and entertainment.

There is nothing wrong with kids being busy—in fact, it is probably preferable to their having excessive time on their hands. But kids' busyness and their caregivers' over-crowded schedules can create a lot of trouble for our kids' need to eat on time. Our too-full days and daily personal decisions can seriously interfere with the natural eating kids need to do in order to avoid weight and eating problems. The school schedule can also hinder kids' body-controlled eating.

Maureen, who teaches seventh grade, heard I was writing a book about preventing obesity and eating disorders in kids. "Oh, my gosh, do we need that!" she exclaimed. "All the fast food and junk food! And kids are getting heavier all the time. You know what? The kids in my third-hour class are always starving—*starving!* They don't have lunch until 1:00, and they are just about fainting in my class. So I let them bring a snack as long as it's a healthy one," she says. "How can they learn anything when they haven't eaten for hours and hours?"

Maureen didn't know about the Feast or Famine Cycle, and we had never discussed the idea that going hungry is bad for kids and leads to weight and eating problems. But having experienced first hand the serious famine situation in her classroom, she had the sense to break the school rule that restricts eating to the cafeteria. Many teachers see the problem, but few understand it or feel at liberty to do anything about it.

Schedules

Our fast-paced lifestyles often leave too little time to eat anything at all at hungry times, much less decent meals. By the time kids' hunger becomes intense, they are often in situations that restrict eating, like the classroom. Famines happen. Many kids are hungry at non-meal times during the day and have to wait hours before a meal is available. Famines happen. Kids often skip breakfast because of lack of time. Neither parents nor kids realize this is a crucial time to fuel-up for the day to avoid the Feast or Famine Cycle. Famines happen.

Yes, famines happen because we are all too busy to eat when we need to.

Making sure kids eat well on time isn't a priority for most people because they don't understand the relationship between going hungry and weight problems. Consequently, kids often miss eating when they need to, or they eat on the run, as if by accident. It follows that the kinds of foods they eat in

90

between "more important things" are not the greatest.

Kelly's mother is a single parent who has to leave for work before her four children catch their school bus. At fourteen, Kelly, the oldest, makes sure her brother and two sisters leave on time. The house is in an uproar most mornings as these kids get ready. Usually their breakfast consists of cold cereal and milk, but Kelly seldom eats even that much because she is rushing around, helping everyone else. Once settled in her seat at school, Kelly realizes she is starving and suffers through until lunch.

Lack of information

Because they haven't learned about the Feast or Famine Cycle, parents don't typically help their kids anticipate their hunger and food needs. They don't realize how important it is to insist on breakfast. Going hungry is seen as benign at worst, therapeutic at best. Often the kids who most need to avoid going hungry—overweight kids and kids with high famine sensitivity—are the ones whose parents are out of touch with their food supply, consciously or unconsciously. Because no one is assessing their extra fuel needs, many, if not most, young athletes regularly work out and perform with inadequate fuel. In general, exercising on an empty stomach is not a concern for parents or coaches and sometimes it is considered an optimal training condition. This kind of ignorance promotes weight and eating disturbances in some kids, sooner or later.

Apart from totally changing our busy schedules to accommodate our kids' fuel needs, what can we adults do to ensure their adequate food availability? The answer is simple but challenging: Plan ahead.

Look at each kid's schedule and fuel needs (if asked, kids will usually tell you about their hungry times) and find ways to get decent food to him or her. Naturally, there are some constraints to work around, such as school breaks, but some simple, practical adjustments can lead to big improvements. Crucial spots are, again, breakfast, mid morning, after school, and hungry times around intense physical activity.

In the previous example, for instance, Kelly's mom had no idea Kelly wasn't eating breakfast until Mom asked. (This is common among teens and parents.) When Mom and Kelly realized how important it was for Kelly to eat well in the morning, they discussed the problem and came up with a plan: prepare each night for the next day, avoiding the hectic morning routine.

Each child set his or her own place at the table and chose a cereal beforehand, eliminating bickering the next day. Clothes were chosen and set out. Dishes could be left until after school.

Mom also asked the kids for other breakfast suggestions. The kids came up with some creative ideas for variety that would work in their situation, including supper leftovers and some choices Mom could fix ahead of time, such as peanut butter sandwiches. These plans made the morning rush much more manageable for Kelly. She found time to eat breakfast most days, and in general her mornings at school went better after the change.

Poor food availability

Related to schedule issues, the third problem that interferes with kids' body-controlled eating is poor food availability. Kids get hungry and there is no food around, or the food available is lower quality—nutrient poor. When hunger strikes, second-rate food is better than no food at all, but poor-quality food still causes a famine and its adaptive responses. Kids need to eat well when they get hungry, but most kids in our country often eat poorly *due to the ready availability of poor-quality food and lack of high-quality food.*

Besides troubleshooting kids' schedules to find famine-creating problem areas, parents and caregivers need to pay careful attention to food availability. Not only do we need to make sure there is food wherever and whenever kids get hungry, but we also need to make sure that food is high-class, good-quality food with plenty of essential nutrients as well as calories. Providing nutritious food is so important that the entire next chapter is devoted to it.

Kids dieting

The traditional eat-less diet deliberately interferes with body-controlled eating. Recent statistics on kids dieting as early as grade school are particularly disturbing—positively terrifying once you understand how undereating can actually instigate lifelong weight and eating problems. Yes, kids are dieting as early as third grade. Most are girls and the vast majority do not have a weight problem. Not yet.

Once kids begin to consciously interfere with their bodies' natural eating instincts by ignoring hunger, eating less than they want, and eating only diet-type foods (e.g., low fat, low calorie), they are unwittingly promoting the Feast or Famine adaptive responses in their bodies. Bulimia and anorexia are now afflicting kids as young as nine. These eating disorders are certainly due to their weight-loss efforts, whatever other issues they may have. These diagnoses simply reflect the war these kids have begun to wage against their bodies' natural eating instincts. The seriousness of the consequences depends on the child's famine sensitivity and the severity and length of the diet.

Peer pressure

Children and adolescents are influenced by their friends in many ways, sometimes for good and sometimes for ill. Girls who begin controlling their food intake may bring their close friends right along with them. Although many of these girls tolerate short periods of undereating (low-calorie) or poor-quality eating (very low-fat, excluding food groups), some can develop eating disorders. Others simply hop on the Feast or Famine Cycle and gradually gain weight as they rebound from their dieting (famine) efforts.

Once kids develop an objective weight problem (from reckless eating, delayed eating and undereating or dieting), their peers often create enormous pressure, especially at school, to avoid eating much of anything. Many overweight kids become so self-conscious about their weight that eating in public is extremely embarrassing. So they avoid it, and the undereating becomes more severe. This type of peer pressure promotes a more severe Feast or Famine Cycle in these kids. Whenever they consciously decide to avoid eating when they are hungry, these kids actively, though unwittingly, set themselves up for even more weight gain and eating struggles.

The things kids get from us besides their looks

We teach our kids amazing things about eating—on purpose and unknowingly. The gems we pass along interfere with body-controlled, instinctive eating. We seem convinced that our bodies are all hell-bent on making us fat if we don't keep careful watch over our appetites. Many of us are fat, so our fears have actually been "proven true." Or so we think. And we pass on our misguided "solutions" to our kids as if we were experts in this area.

There are many ways adults communicate their own attitudes, beliefs, prejudices, superstitions, and fears about food to kids in their care. Some are obvious, others extremely subtle.

- We pass along to our kids our poor eating habits, resulting in weight/eating struggles.
- We model food avoidance and fears of becoming fat, especially to young women, from infancy onward.
- We can seldom hide from our kids our prejudices

about overweight people.

- Sometimes we openly express these prejudices as a means of motivating our kids to avoid getting fat.

Adults who have weight/eating issues of their own are bound to share their food anxieties and struggles with the children in their lives.

The family sets initial body-image standards, but kids are also influenced by propaganda in the press—at times in a stronger way. But parents' own unrealistic or distorted body image standards ill equip them to support kids in battling "The Thin Ideal" of the American culture. Misinformation can interfere with kids' instinctive eating, so it's essential that people who feed kids get the straight scoop on natural eating and healthy body image.

Destructive messages we send our kids

1. It's OK (even beneficial) to ignore hunger and go without food because there are "right times" to be hungry and to eat based on schedules and routines.
1. It's OK to ignore fullness signals and eat more food than you want/need because of other people's ideas of what and how much you should eat.
2. Some foods are "good," some foods are "bad" based on diet fads and prejudices.
3. There are "right amounts" of certain foods to eat based on other people's ideas.
4. Eating "too much," in and of itself, will make you fat. Self-control is the only ingredient necessary to maintain a normal body weight.

How do we send these strong, unhealthy messages? By what we say day after day about our own or our kids' eating behavior. Over time, these reinforced messages harden into beliefs that may set kids up for weight problems and eating struggles for a lifetime. Let's consider each of these destructive message examples.

Message #1: It's OK to ignore hunger and go without food.

This message tops the list because it sets the stage for the Feast or Famine Cycle. Because body-controlled eating depends on kids staying tuned in to their hunger signals, this approach is the major culprit that tempts kids away from their natural eating instincts and sets them up for disaster. Here are some things we may say that send the wrong message:

"You can't be hungry, you had a snack an hour ago!"

> *The adult is really saying:* That's not hunger you're feeling, and if it is, you should ignore it because you just ate something only an hour ago. According to my objective calculations, there is no way you could really need to eat again so soon, and I am the expert on your body's need for food, not you.
> *Conclusions kids make:* Even though what I'm feeling sure feels like hunger, it must be something else because of those chips I had. My mom knows when I'm ready to eat better than I do, so I'd better shut up and wait until she says I'm hungry or I'll make her mad again.

"You're hungry? Well, supper isn't nearly ready, so go back outside and play. I'll tell you when it's time to be hungry."

> *The adult is really saying:* It doesn't matter that you're hungry now because now is not the time that food is ready. The time to be hungry is when the food is ready. It won't hurt you to wait and get some exercise in the meantime. Then you'll be plenty hungry for supper, and maybe you'll finish your meal for

a change.

Conclusions kids make: My hunger doesn't matter. What matters is when the food is ready. I should ignore feeling hungry unless food is ready to eat. It's a good idea to play hard when you are hungry but there is no food. Other people know best when you should be hungry and eat.

"If you had eaten all your lunch, you wouldn't be hungry again now. I don't care how hungry you are, I'm not digging out a snack. Maybe next time you'll finish your lunch."

The adult is really saying: Your hunger doesn't count now because you left some lunch uneaten earlier. Hunger that is caused by "irresponsible eating" (i. e., not stuffing yourself at mealtime) is hunger that should be punished. You should feel guilty for inconveniencing me by getting hungry at the wrong time. Ignore it.

Conclusions kids make: Leaving food uneaten at a previous meal should cancel out your next hunger signals. I don't deserve to eat again when I feel hungry because I didn't eat what my day-care lady thought I should at lunch. Next time, if I finish my lunch, I can have a snack later. I think.

"Hungry? A little hunger won't hurt you. I never ate breakfast before school when I was a kid and I grew up big and strong. Hunger builds character!"

The adult is really saying: It's perfectly normal and healthy to go hungry, even when there's food around to eat. Almost everyone does it. None are worse for the wear. In fact, going hungry is one good way to grow up into a strong person like Mom or Dad.

Conclusions kids make: This hunger feels like pain, but I guess it isn't the kind of pain to worry about. After all, Dad skipped breakfast. He was a great football player in high school and look at him now. You'd never guess he ever missed a meal in his life! I wonder what "character" is.

"You're hungry? We'll be eating dinner at Grandma's in two hours so you'll just have to wait. You know how important it is to bring a big appetite to Grandma's!"

> *The adult is really saying:* It's not only OK to ignore hunger for hours, it is required by the social calendar and family expectations. Other people's feelings and expectations take precedence over individual hunger signals.
>
> *Conclusions kids make:* Now is definitely not the time to feel this hungry because it's a long way (timewise) to Grandma's house. Eating a lot of Grandma's food is the most important thing about going there because she is happier and loves you more the more you eat. And if you're not extra hungry, she's really disappointed. So, I'd better wait and eat a lot there.

"I'm absolutely starved! I haven't eaten all day. I've been so busy!"

> *The adult is really saying:* It's OK to skip eating during the day because of a crowded schedule. In fact, you can take a certain pride in this stoic behavior, which requires willpower and stamina. It's positively heroic.
>
> *Conclusions kids make:* It's normal to skip eating altogether when you get really busy.

" Your friends are waiting outside for you. Never mind lunch—you can always eat later. Summer won't last forever, you know."

> *The adult is really saying:* When there's social pressure,

eating is not important. Whether a kid eats sooner or later makes no difference as long as he's taking advantage of his sports and social opportunities. *Conclusions kids make:* Don't worry about being hungry when you have a chance to play with your friends. Ignore it and get out with your friends.

Message #2: It's OK to ignore fullness signals.

The important thing to remember about this message is that usually kids can't ignore their fullness signals. Overeating repulses them unless they are on the Feast or Famine Cycle. So admonitions to ignore fullness and keep eating often go unheeded, causing friction between parents/caregivers and kids. Adults can avoid this friction by understanding the way body-controlled eating works.

"You can't be full. You've hardly touched your food!"

The adult is really saying: I know more about your being full than you do, and I know you're not full. So, ignore that whatever the feeling is you are having, and keep eating.

Conclusions kids make: Although I feel full, it isn't possible because I've only eaten a little food. This full feeling might be something else because Mom is sure I am not full.

"You can leave the table when you have finished eating all your food."

The adult is really saying: Fullness happens outside the body, not inside. The signal to stop eating comes from a clean plate, not from the body feeling full and wanting to stop eating.

Conclusions kids make: Even though I am stuffed, the signal for being done with a meal is the clean plate. I have to ignore this aversion to food that I feel and keep eating in order to be free from the table. My parents know what is best when it comes to eating.

"You're not that full. Here, have another helping. It's your favorite."

> *The adult is really saying:* Keep eating the foods you love, whether or not you are already full. Who knows when you may get another chance to have them?
> *Conclusions kids make:* I guess I can squeeze in one more helping. We don't have it that often so I might as well enjoy as much of it as I can. You can always eat a few more bites of something special.

"Mother made this dish especially for you and you only took a few bites. Eat the rest or you'll hurt her feelings."

> *The adult is really saying:* It doesn't matter that you only wanted a few bites. What matters is Mother's (and my) feelings. So stuff this food down, and we'll all be happy.
> *Conclusions kids make:* It's best to ignore feeling full and eat for the sake of other people's feelings. How much I eat affects the happiness of others, so I must keep this in mind because love is important.

"This is a very expensive restaurant. You have hardly touched your food. That is wasting a lot of money, Honey, so finish it up."

> *The adult is really saying:* The fact that you do not want to eat any more food is not the issue here. Money is the issue. Ignore your body's full signals and give us our money's worth.
> *Conclusions kids make:* Great restaurant food is a waste of money unless you eat every last bite, regard-

less of your hunger level. So, stuff it down, whether you like it or not, or you may not get a chance to enjoy eating out again.

Message #3: Some foods are "good" and some foods are "bad."

This message has nothing to do with the objective value of various foods. It has to do with our dietary prejudices and the fads adults may follow dealing with their own weight or health issues. You'll recognize some of the latest fads in these examples, and perhaps you can think of some prejudices you've fostered.

"I can't have bananas—too many carbohydrates!"

> *The adult is really saying:* Bananas are intrinsically fattening because of the carbohydrate content.
> *Conclusions kids make:* Bananas are bad for you because they have something in them that is harmful, called kahrdovibrates—whatever they are.

"I used to love eggs, but I can't have them since I'm watching my fat."

> *Adult is really saying:* Even though I enjoy eating eggs, they are bad if you have to control your fat intake.
> *Conclusions kids make:* If you don't want to get fat, you can't eat eggs even if you love them.

"On this diet I can eat all the vegetables I want. But I have to limit fruits, bread, pasta, potatoes, meat and dairy products."

> *Adult is really saying:* Eating foods you don't particularly like is best on a diet.
> *Conclusions kids make:* Foods that taste best must be bad for you.

"You didn't eat your fish. Fish is good for you. It has omega 3 fatty acids!"

> *The adult is really saying:* I am trying to provide a balanced diet here, and you are not cooperating! Fish has essential nutrients that I just read an article about and you need these nutrients, so eat up, like it or not!
> *Conclusions kids make:* Whether or not you like a food, you should eat it because it has something in it that is good for you. In the case of fish, this is fatty something, which is really weird because usually, fatty stuff is bad for you. Food is confusing, and you sure can't trust your own taste buds to know what you should eat.

"The book said any kind of meat or fish is OK on this diet. Any protein food is good for me and will help me lose weight."

> *The adult is really saying:* Certain foods are acceptable and promote weight loss. Protein foods in general fall into this category.
> *Conclusions kids make:* Some foods are magical because they have pro-teen, whatever that is.

"If people would just stop eating meat, there wouldn't be so many fat people."

> *The adult is really saying:* The way to avoid getting fat is by becoming a vegetarian.
> *Conclusions kids make:* Meat makes you fat, so stay away from meat!

Message #4: There are "right amounts" to eat of certain foods.

Adults seem to have extraordinary gifts of knowledge when it comes to their kids' eating. One of these gifts involves "knowing" how much of what foods is the right amount for a particular kid to eat on any given occasion. This wisdom is, of course, imposed from outside the kid's own body. And adults often offer this wisdom when the kid's body signals have caused him to avoid the food altogether or to stop eating a particular food. Kids must violate their own natural body-controlled eating instincts if they are going to submit to the adult's "higher intelligence." After all, what does a child's body know, anyway?

"You didn't finish your potatoes. Take three more bites and you may be excused."

> *The Adult is really saying:* Don't pay any attention to that signal to stop eating that you feel. Your body does not know the right amount of potatoes to eat at this moment, and you need someone smarter than your body to tell you how much to eat. The exact amount of potatoes you should eat is three additional bites. Your freedom is contingent upon your eating a certain amount of a certain type of food.
> *Conclusions kids make:* I must not be done with my potatoes because they are not gone. Dad knows I should eat three more bites to be really finished and he won't let me out of here until I eat up.

"No, you can't have more corn. You didn't finish your chicken."

> *The Adult is really saying:* You aren't allowed to enjoy more of the food you like until you finish eating all the particular food I think you should eat. When you eat all the other food you have left, I will give you more of the food you want, but not before.
> *Conclusions kids make:* Ignore the I don't want any more chicken sensation you have. You are supposed to

eat the whole piece before you want any other food. It doesn't matter what foods you prefer or in what amounts. The important thing is, eat the amount of whatever foods other people tell you. Then and only then you may get more of what you want to eat.

"One peanut butter sandwich is enough. You shouldn't eat two sandwiches at a time. It's a basic principle of life."

The adult is really saying: There are definite, objective amounts of food that are proper to eat, and one sandwich is enough food, period. Eating more than one sandwich is not right, no matter what you want. Life is full of these important disciplines.

Conclusions kids make: Hunger for a second sandwich is no indication that that's what you should eat. You can't trust your body. So ignore those signals and go with the advice of other people who know better than you how to limit your eating.

"You ate that whole bunch of grapes? You're going to turn into a grape if you keep that up."

The adult is really saying: I'm shocked that you ate an entire bunch of grapes. That must be thirty or forty grapes! All that sugar! All those carbs! This is how fat people get started.

Conclusions kids make: I must have been crazy to eat all those grapes. Even if I thought I just really like grapes, I'm just kidding myself. If I let myself eat all I want I will turn into the foods I really like. So I'd better start limiting those grapes before my skin turns purple.

"You may each have two pieces of pizza, and that's it. Each piece has 175 calories and 12 grams of fat. You can't just eat

all you want."

> *The adult is really saying:* You have to learn to control
> portions while you are young. You might as well learn
> about the calorie and fat contents of foods so you
> won't have to suffer through life being overweight
> like I am.
> *Conclusions kids make:* Pizza is scary. It is fattening.
> You have to be careful about eating pizza and never,
> ever go ahead and eat without a plan. I'm not sure
> what would happen, but it would definitely be bad.

Message #5: Eating "too much," in and of itself, will make you fat.

Adults communicate this message to kids in many ways
because most people believe it is true. Although overeating is
a factor in obesity, it is only a part of the picture. Perhaps it
is the most obvious and logical promoter of weight problems,
but the stimulus for overeating—undereating—is just as significant, perhaps more so. The equation is incomplete without understanding the famine stimulus, and kids learn the
same half picture of obesity that their parents and caregivers
have acquired. This keeps adults and children alike focused
on trying to control symptoms rather than supporting quality
body-controlled eating.

"Two bowls of cereal and toast and juice! Keep that up and you'll start packing on the pounds."

> *The adult is really saying:* A substantial meal will lead
> you down that steep road to a fat body. Never mind
> that you want it—that your hunger is substantial. This
> amount of food is just too much, period. Pay atten-
> tion to my voice of wisdom and ignore your body's
> urge to eat. What does your body know, anyway?
> *Conclusions kids make:* Wow, I must be eating too

much. But I was so hungry this morning. Well, I'd better start watching it because Mom should know. She's been watching her weight for as long as I can remember.

"All this after-school snacking and you're headed for a weight problem. Look at me. I got this way from snacking. You want to look like me?"

> *The adult is really saying:* If you keep eating after school like this, you are going to get fat. I believe between-meal snacking led to my weight problem because the last program I was on emphasized avoiding unscheduled snacking. I am afraid for you.
> *Conclusions kids make:* There is something mysteriously dangerous about between-meal eating that leads to weight problems. Food eaten at meal times is OK, but food eaten between meals makes bodies fat. Avoid eating unless it is mealtime, hungry or not—or else.

"You have been eating nonstop on this trip. This will catch up to you. How do you think Freddie got so fat?"

> *The adult is really saying:* Eating a lot of food may not make you fat right away, but eventually it most certainly will.
> *Conclusions kids make:* Eating "nonstop" (whatever that means) is dangerous. Ignore the hunger that makes you want to eat, and you will avoid the sad fate of all the Freddies in the world.

"Why do you think Aunt Nellie is so fat? Because she eats too much, of course. She has diabetes, too. You'd think she would try harder."

The adult is really saying: Aunt Nellie eats too much all the time and it is making her sick. Apparently she doesn't care.

Conclusions kids make: I wonder why Aunt Nellie doesn't try harder to stop eating so much, especially with her diabetes. It's OK to criticize sick people.

"Sally has gotten huge! She should just stop eating altogether for a year and she'd be about normal."

The adult is really saying: Fat people get fat by eating too much, and they should be able to get back to slim by not eating—altogether if possible. So, if you have a weight problem, just stop eating and that should fix it.

Conclusions kids make: It's OK to ridicule fat people. They could easily fix their problem by not eating anything. I wonder why more fat people don't do that. They sure would feel better, and people would stop making fun of them.

The new message to kids

Once we understand the whole picture of obesity and eating disorders, we will stop teaching our kids superstitions and half-truths about food and eating. Instead, we can give our kids true information, information that supports their instinctive eating. We can teach our kids to trust their bodies—their body signals—for fuel needs and fullness. We can encourage them to pay attention to their hunger and always eat good food when they get hungry. But there is more we adults can and must do to support body-controlled eating in our children and teenagers. We must provide good food.

Parents' #1 Job

6

The food we provide for our kids to eat is key to their diet quality.

One of the main jobs of child rearing is supplying nutritious food. But many parents don't know how because they don't know what high-quality food is. They may have grown up with a poor-quality diet fraught with famines. So the idea of providing good-quality food at home may seem mysterious, even impossible, to manage. It's not. The food supply in the environment consists of three things:

    1. what foods are available (quality)

    2. how much food is available (quantity)

    3. when foods are available for eating (timing).

The food supply determines how bodies adapt with eating, appetite, and weight changes, including the five adaptive responses to famines. Kids who get plenty of quality food on demand do not need to store extra fat for surviving famines. And these kids generally exhibit normal, balanced appetites, healthy metabolic rates, and plenty of energy for physical activity.

When famines occur only occasionally and are not severe, kids' bodies don't need to prepare for them with adaptive mechanisms that promote an excess internal food supply of fat. Without the need for famine protection, kids' bodies are free to adapt to the optimal food supply with optimal body weight.

When food availability is optimal and eating is governed by body signals, excess appetite and weight problems will not occur. It would simply not be adaptive in such an environment. So, once kids' eating is body controlled, for the most part, and quantity famines much more rare, this positive food supply is the next necessary thing to provide if we are going to eliminate quality famines and prevent weight and eating problems from developing in our kids. This simply means that we make available to our kids good-quality food, not poor-quality food.

The food supply

A mother of four raised her hand at my seminar and asked me how she could get her kids to stop eating so many cookies. She was serious.

I suggested that she stop buying cookies.

"You mean, don't have any cookies at all?"

"Yes," I replied.

"Well, I couldn't do that," she said, incredulously. "We have to have some cookies. They're the kids' favorite snack!"

Many parents think this way. They have become so accustomed to serving their kids poor-quality (though tasty) foods that they can't imagine eliminating them. I think some genuinely fear what their kids might do if their favorite lower quality snacks and treats disappeared. Just as adults do, kids get used to the way things are in their lives, and they tend to resist change at first. But eventually, and usually sooner than adults, kids adjust whether they like it or not. As long as the changes we impose upon our kids are not abusive and are done with the kids' welfare in mind, kids generally—if not quietly—accept new patterns and expectations within a few weeks. It's helpful to keep this in mind during their protest phase.

Is it absolutely necessary to eliminate these not-so-great foods in order for your kids to avoid obesity and eating disorders? No, it's not. If your kids are not famine sensitive and almost always eat on time, poor-quality food is not evil, nor can it single handedly cause weight and eating problems.

So why urge every kid caregiver to restrict the availability of these foods? I think kids should eat the best food they can at home because they're likely to eat poorer-quality food when they're away. This is a fact unless you have an extremely unusual kid. Let me say it another way:

When hungry, kids will eat quality foods they like
that they find around the house, and
kids will not eat foods that are not there.

These are such a profound statements that they merit further discussion. Let's look at the first part first:

When hungry, kids will eat quality foods they like
that they find around the house.

This statement is so simple that it seems almost moronic to explain. But, as with most simple but profound ideas, there are some important things to say about it just the same. Let's dissect it to understand all its subtle implications.

When hungry

Hungry babies, children and adolescents don't have to be forced or even encouraged to eat. Hungry kids want to eat good food they like when they are hungry. The only times adults have to coerce them to eat is when they are not hungry or they don't like the food.

Forcing a kid to eat when he isn't hungry is abusive. Abuse breaks down trust in a relationship, so forcing kids to eat when the kids aren't hungry damages the relationship between the kid and the adult doing the forcing. Usually, adults who insist that kids eat regardless of their hunger level are genuinely concerned about their kids' nutritional needs. But right motives don't excuse wrong behavior.

Concerned parents might better simply state their concern: "You say you're not hungry, but you hardly ate any breakfast and it's after noon. I'm afraid you won't get enough good food to stay healthy and grow up strong. If you're sure you're really not hungry yet, your body must be doing OK for now."

Sometimes kids refuse good food they like because they are getting sick, and a depressed appetite precedes other symptoms. Parents admit that loss of appetite is the signal they have come to identify with an impending illness in their kids. This is another reason to respect kids' body-controlled eating patterns.

Most kids will refuse to eat foods they don't like and this can drive the adults in their lives crazy. Parents can keep encouraging their kids to try new foods, but never force it. You'll likely reap the same consequences that result from forcing kids to eat when they are not hungry.

kids . . .

This term is more inclusive than you might imagine at first. Naturally, it refers to children, from infancy through the late teens. But the fact is, this statement may apply to any person living within a household—mothers, fathers, grandparents, kids in their 20s and 30s, aunts, uncles, and nannies. One might even venture to say that all people of all ages will eat the foods they find where they live. So *it is impractical to provide a high-quality food supply for your kids and a lower quality food supply for anyone else living in your household at the same time.*

For example, Mark and Rita want to improve the food quality for their kids, but Mark does not want to give up his favorite football game snack—potato chips and dip. Rita does not want to give up her favorite treat either—ice cream with Oreo cookies. Can't they hide these favorites from their kids? Not likely.

Besides, kids have a strong sense of fairness. While you're touting the many advantages of their sticking with healthy, real foods, they'll know you're being a hypocrite right under your own roof. Parents who want to make big changes in food quality at home should bite the bullet themselves and *demonstrate* high-quality eating to their kids at the same time they're talking about it.

will eat quality foods they like . . .

We've already established the fact that hungry kids will eat good food that's available. The words *quality foods* and *they like* are the key phrases to providing the optimal food availability for your kids. We'll get to them in a minute, but before we get to specific food quality and kids' food preferences, let's finish the first phrase.

that they find around the house

Kids eat the foods they find in their homes—in the cupboards, in the refrigerator, on the countertops, in the freezer. It's so simple. If it's there, and kids like it, they'll eat it. This makes the task of controlling kids' food quality at home extremely simple. If you want them to eat it, buy it. If you don't want them to eat it, don't buy it. Period.

"Well, what about Troy's house? He'll just go over there for cookies," one mother protests.

But I'm not talking about the neighbor's food supply, I'm talking about yours. Let's not give up just because everyone doesn't understand these concepts as we do.

Kids will not eat food that isn't there

By now you're probably chuckling or irritated at my overstating of this point. But I have discovered that it needs overstating because parents and others who supply food to kids tend to leave their common sense outside the grocery store door. They seem more concerned with the cheers and smiles they may get from kids discovering their favorite goodies at home than they are with the health and nutritional needs of those kids. And they also seem to be willing to set themselves up for fights over treats vs. good food, spoiled appetites, and cranky moods from high-sugar, lower quality eating.

Let's assume that you want to provide excellent food for your kids at all times. Where do you start? You start at a very simple spot: *the grocery store.* Buy plenty of high-quality ingredients and foods that kids like. Then work consistently to make these foods available, day in and day out. That's it in a nutshell. Now let's figure out how to do it.

If not at birth, then now

The best time to change the household food supply to high quality is ASAP. Don't waste any time or emotional energy feeling badly or beating yourself up for keeping junk food and sweets and treats around all these years, even if your kids are big junk-food eaters and are overweight. You haven't had the information or the resolve to do better. Now you do. No matter what ages your kids are, it is not too late to improve their diet—probably dramatically.

It is so important to get kids eating good food on time as early in their lives as possible because *kids become accustomed to the foods that they are fed and learn to expect and prefer these tastes and varieties of foods.* They also get used to eating instinctively (on demand) and tend not to tolerate going hungry very well, which is a very good thing.

For example, two-year-old Rose and her five-year-old brother, Brian, have always eaten instinctively, and their parents have been providing excellent quality food from day one. Consequently, Rose and Brian are accustomed to eating broccoli and salads and beans and brown rice and chicken breast and fish fillets and spaghetti and whole grain breads and cereals without sugar coatings. Naturally, they have their preferences and dislike some foods, but on the whole, they eat good-quality food on demand at home and even tend to prefer better quality foods when away. Naturally, these two children are both at their ideal weight.

What are high-quality foods?

High-quality foods (I also call them real foods) are rather easy to identify. First, quality foods tend to be meal-type foods—typically eaten during a regular meal. But some real foods can lose their high-quality status when they are prepared with too much sugar or fat. For example, cereals are generally real foods, but when they are sugar coated, they lose their place in the quality foods category. Sugar has calories but no other nutrients. This is why we call sugar "empty calories."

Another example of a terrific real food is potatoes. Potatoes taste great and they're loaded with nutrients. They can be prepared dozens of different ways and still qualify as real food. But when they are deep fried into french fries, potatoes lose their high-nutrient profile. They end up soaked in fat—another source of empty calories.

To give you confidence in providing quality food to your kids, here's a complete Real Food List, which contains most of the foods we Americans feed our families. And remember, preparation counts. It can even cancel out the quality of a real food.

REAL FOODS
Quality foods you can confidently feed your kids anytime:

Breads, grains, cereals
Whole-grain foods in this category are better, unless your
  kids don't like or tolerate them
all breads (excluding breakfast pastries, donuts, etc.)
bagels, English muffins, pretzels, crackers
all unsweetened cold or hot cereals
  (sugar is OK as a condiment)
pasta, all types
rice (including brown, wild and white)
all sandwiches made with real food fillings
dumplings, stuffing
muffins, waffles, pancakes, French toast, etc.
pizza with cheese, any vegetables, lean pizza meat
potato chips, baked

Nuts, seeds, legumes
seeds of all types
nuts of all kinds
peanut butter, almond butter, other seed/nut spreads
beans of all kinds

Fruits and vegetables
all fruits
all vegetables
vegetable-based dishes, such as oriental stir-fry,
  vegetable casseroles
fruit jams and jellies
juices (100 % unsweetened fruit or vegetable juice)
salads made from vegetables and/or fruits
soups made from real foods

Dairy
milk (whole or fat reduced, depending on age and

individual needs)
cheese, all types
cottage cheese
yogurt, preferably sweetened with fruit
cream as a condiment
sour cream
cream cheese
milk-based, cream-based soups
eggs

Meat, poultry, seafood
beef (lean cuts)
chicken
fish (all types)
turkey, other poultry
ground beef, extra lean
pork (lean cuts)
shellfish
soups, stews

Fats, spreads
butter
vegetable oils

Condiments
mustard, vinegar, relishes
fresh or dried herbs, spices
sugar, syrup
ketchup, barbecue sauce, hot sauce, salsa
steak sauces
fruit dips, Veggie dips
salad dressings
jelly, jams, preserves

Beverages

unsweetened fruit or vegetable juice, juice pops
sugar-free beverages, diet pop, powdered drinks (not
    so great for kids–limit)
hot chocolate
milk (white, chocolate, strawberry-flavored)
water

If you don't know what a "lean cut" of pork is or whether or
not a cereal is presweetened, ask people at the grocery store.
The butcher can point out the leaner cuts of meat and various
percentages of fat. Staff from the deli or fresh foods sections
can usually help you read labels to determine sugar content as
well as other ingredients. It's safe to say that a product listing
sugar, corn syrup or brown sugar as the first or second ingredient is not a real food.

Other places to get information about food quality are
the library, bookstore, or Internet. There are dozens of books
about nutrition to choose from. The only drawback to these
books is that they tend to be more complicated than practical.
Sometimes, adults get so much detailed information from
these books that they lose sight of the big picture—providing
quality food to kids whenever they are hungry. Instead of
details on proteins, carbohydrates, fats and vitamins, the most
helpful information contains general guidelines for food quality and balance. So choose a book that is simple, easy to follow, and practical. Sample menus are especially helpful for
adults looking to improve their kids' eating quality. You'll find
these elements in the appendix of this book.

OK, so those are the quality foods to choose from at
the grocery store. But what about the other foods—the ones
our kids want, such as cookies, candy, ice cream, brownies,
and cake? Where do poor-quality but tasty kid treats fit in?
Are these foods always bad? Can kids ever have foods not on
the "real" list?

These are good questions, so let's start with the first one: What about the other foods, the treats my kids really like?

There are two other food groups that may help you decide how to handle these other foods in your kid's diet. The second group of foods is called "borderline foods" because these foods fall between the high-quality foods and the lower quality category. Borderline foods are real foods that have particularly high fat and/or sugar content. These foods are not without merit nutritionally, but they are definitely not optimal for kids to eat every day:

BORDERLINE FOODS

> deep-fried anything
> potato chips, nacho chips, any fried snack chips
> french fries
> most fast foods, except single-patty hamburgers and
>   "lite" menu options
> sweet rolls, pastries
> bacon, sausage, processed meats (salami, bologna)
> pudding, custard
> presweetened cereals
> pizza with high-fat meats
>   (sausage, pepperoni, hamburger)

There are some very popular kid items on this list, but these foods should be the exception rather than the daily fare for most kids. The quality isn't there although the taste satisfaction sure is. These foods, reserved for special occasions, won't threaten a kid's diet health when only available now and then.

The third food category is called "pleasure foods" for obvious reasons. Kids eat these foods primarily for the taste hit they get. These foods have calories, but typically little else in the way of nutrients. They are designed with taste in mind, and generally they fill the bill.

PLEASURE FOODS

cakes, frosting
chocolate anything
candy, candy bars
cookies and bars
fudge
betties, cobblers, strudel, etc.
pies, dessert pastries
ice cream, ice milk, sherbet, frozen yogurt
ice cream concoctions, malts, shakes
sweet toppings, ice cream and desert syrups
soda pop, punch, Kool-Aid, all sugar-based drinks
fruit "drinks" made with some fruit juice
   plus sugar/fructose

Special-occasion pleasure foods are fine but only for very special occasions, no more than once a week at home as a guideline. Remember, pleasure foods are everywhere your kids are (away from home) and kids will gobble or guzzle them whenever they can. Perhaps the main problem with borderline and pleasure foods is that they satisfy appetites so well that kids don't have room left for the good stuff.

In fact, kids may lose their taste for higher quality food once they get used to the lower quality, high-fat and high-sugar foods. Baked potatoes with butter or sour cream may become unappealing to a child who gets french fries at McDonald's every other day. So what's a mother to do? Stop visiting Ronald so often.

Cravings for sweets

Some parents say their kids simply can't do without sweets because their cravings are so strong. Their kids prefer sweets so much of the time that these parents are convinced that there is something about sweets and junk food their children need. They could be right. Children and adolescents who don't get enough quality calories on a regular basis develop an adaptive need for fat-producing foods. This is why they crave them.

Fat-producing foods are typically high in sugar and/or fat and are designed to efficiently produce extra fat to protect these reckless eaters from starvation. Remember, cravings are correlated to physiological needs. Kids who want candy and chips and ice cream frequently have good reason. They aren't eating enough good stuff. So, the remedy for the sweet tooth is simple: Feed the hunger with the best quality food that will satisfy.

When kids' hunger is strong, they are more likely to want sweets or junk food. These foods are easier to digest and the fuel gets right into the bloodstream. This relieves hunger pangs fast, but the relief may be short lived because these foods burn up fast too. So, in an emergency, it's fine to offer very hungry kids candy or other sweets, but obtain real food ASAP so they get good nutrients too. Remember to keep the emergencies to a minimum by carrying real food with you in the car and anticipating your kids' fuel needs away from home.

If kids ask for sweets or poor-quality food when real food is available, you have decisions to make. Your choice should be based on each kid's eating pattern and regular diet quality. For example, a kid who eats good-quality food most of the time and is definitely body-controlled will not suffer ill effects from occasional indulgences. But other kids need guidance and support in making better choices consistently. These are the kids who prefer borderline and pleasure foods as a rule. Adults can help these kids learn to satisfy their sweet tooth without sacrificing real food nutrition.

Eleven-year-old Jesse begs his mother to get him an ice cream sundae on their way home from hockey practice. Mom knows Jesse had a candy bar after school, before practice. He didn't touch the sandwich she'd packed for a snack.

"I know you're starving, Jess, but you need better quality food after the workout you just had," she says. "How about peanut butter and jelly on toast, and some hot chocolate?"

"Mom, I really want a sundae! Please?"

"Not today. It's important to stick with good food. And remember, you're an athlete," she responds.

"OK. The coach said something about eating right. Maybe it'll help me score!"

Always try substituting a real food (one with a higher fat and protein content, or even a borderline food) for a pleasure food when you can. This has two positive effects. First, in the long run, kids' food quality will be better; less lower quality food, more nutrient-rich food. Second, as you help kids adjust their food choices toward higher quality foods, kids are learning how to do this for themselves.

Cravings for sweets and rich food are almost always signals that kids need fuel, period. The goal is to improve kids' diets by encouraging them to eat high-quality food as much as possible. This means raising the standard for food quality in your home every day.

Now that we know the good food from the not-so-good food, where do parents and caregivers start in order to feed their kids better? First, take an honest look at how you're feeding them now. Jot down on a piece of paper what and when and where your kids ate today. Then look at yesterday and think back to the day before. If you're not sure where, when, or what they ate, ask them. Then compare this three-day list with the food lists you just read, and see how you're doing.

There's probably room for improvement, right? Here's where you start:

Food availability at home

Look in your refrigerator, freezer, and cupboards for foods
that qualify as real foods kids like. Make a list of these foods.
Then ask your kids the following:

- What foods do you like on this real food list?
- What real food dishes are your favorites for each
  meal?
- What real foods would you like to have ready to eat
  when you come home from school?
- What are your favorite fruits? Vegetables?
- Would you like fruit or vegetables cut up for a
  snack? With dip?
- Do you prefer peanut butter toast or bagels with
  cream cheese?
- What fruit juices are your favorites?
- What real foods do you prefer for snacks?

If your kids are older, is there something they can microwave,
such as a pot pie or mini pizza? Who plans supper? Do
meals at home need a little more thought in advance? Ask
your kids for their input, and you may get some surprises.

Some families simply don't have time to fix much of a
dinner every night. But with even a little extra thought, meals
can become better quality and less stressful to make. For
example, most kids like spaghetti or other pasta dishes. It's
almost as easy to make two or more batches at once, and save
the extra quantity for the next night or the night after that.
Other leftovers can be frozen in individual servings for the
future. Then all that needs to be done on the subsequent
spaghetti night is to add a quick veggie or salad and some
garlic toast (in the toaster).

Even preparation of grilled or sauteed chicken breasts,
pork chops, or steak can be doubled, saving half for another
dinner. Fresh steamed vegetables (or frozen, cooked in the
microwave), provide quick and easy accompaniments.

Prewashed greens turn into a healthy salad in two minutes, potatoes can be microwaved in a few minutes, white rice in fifteen. Be creative. Buy prepackaged stir-fry vegetables, and precut meats to save preparation time. The extra money is well worth it. Eating out is much more expensive. Rationalize any extra grocery spending you do with that reminder. *Make fixing a decent meal for dinner as easy as possible,* and you'll find you're making good dinners much more often. Lunches and breakfasts follow the same rules, but breakfast is especially tricky because of the workweek time crunch.

Making breakfast a high priority in your house

Because famine prevention is the goal of your food availability improvements, your number one target must be breakfast. *Every child and adolescent needs—**needs**—to eat a quality breakfast every single day.* This fact cannot be emphasized too much to parents who want to prevent obesity and eating disorders in their kids. Famines begin early in the day for kids who skip their first meal. Then the kids often get caught up in make-up eating the rest of the day.

What do your kids want for breakfast? Maybe it's something unconventional, such as pizza or leftover dinner food. Maybe they'd heat up frozen waffles or Chinese egg rolls. Whatever they want that's real food (or even borderline food—morning is the best time to pack in the higher calorie fatty foods), buy it and figure out how to make sure they'll get it into their bodies before they go out the door in the morning. It's as simple as that. If they're not hungry in the morning, you can't force them to eat, but encourage it. We'll talk about this problem in the next chapter, "Get Kids to Eat Good Food on Time."

What about McDonald's?

Fast food is a big part of our fast-lane culture. We simply

must eat on the run at times. Is this going to make or break kids' nutritional health? Will eating at fast-food restaurants make my kid fat because of the quality famines? Let's go back to the basic ideas about preventing the development of weight and eating problems. Kids' bodies have the potential to adjust to *famines* (undereating, poor-quality eating, delayed eating) with *five adaptive responses:* increased appetite, depressed metabolic rate, cravings for sweets and fatty foods, preoccupation with food and eating, and avoidance of activity. The thing that makes a kid's individual response to famines unique is his or her *famine sensitivity*.

Varying levels of famine sensitivity explain why some kids can eat recklessly, delay eating, and eat a lot of poor-quality food without ever developing a weight or eating problem. The overall poor quality (high fat content) of the food at fast-food restaurants does not, by itself, make kids fat. Many kids who eat often at fast-food restaurants never develop weight problems because they either have low famine sensitivity and/or they never famine by going hungry.

Low famine sensitivity is a genetic gift. But if kids *never famine*, which is an eating behavior, that makes the crucial difference. Kids who don't famine do not have to do make-up eating. Their metabolisms are not depressed. They remain active. Fast foods, though not the best quality foods, do not, by themselves, cause obesity and eating problems in kids. Let me say that again: *Fast foods do not, by themselves, cause obesity and eating problems in kids.*

Are fast foods all right, then? Although not the culprit in obesity (famines are the culprit), most fast food (FF) is still lower quality food because of its higher fat content. There are better choices among the national FF chains and it is important to check each restaurant's nutritional stats to decide which ones you will offer your kids. If you know you will still go to McDonald's or Burger King, decide beforehand what the best options are. Shoot for no more than about 30 percent fat in any item. The sandwiches at Subway are all fairly healthy and the fresh vegetables (if your kids will eat them) are great. At first, if you plan to control their options, prepare your kids in advance. Initially, ordering the best sandwiches that they like and some quality drinks for them is probably best. It eliminates a lot of hassle. Hungry kids will eat the food you provide even if they don't get a perfect choice.

Because most kids experience famines sometimes, the famine-sensitive ones can easily do high-fat make-up eating at fast-food restaurants. This may lead to weight and eating problems, but again, the lower quality food is not the problem by itself. It is a symptom of the problem. The problem is the famine experience—delayed eating, undereating, going hungry, and poor-quality foods in general.

If you focus on eliminating the famines and keep food quality high in general, fast-food visits once or twice a week should not be a problem. How, exactly do you do this in everyday family life? What does "eliminating the famines" look like? And how do you get your kids to cooperate with a program that seriously threatens all their favorite treats and snack foods? We'll discuss these questions in Part Three.

Part Three:

*How Can We Prevent
Future Food Issues
for Our Kids?*

Get Kids to Eat Good Food on Time

7

Find ways to motivate kids to eat well when they need to.

Motivating children and adolescents to change their eating habits when they are not concerned about their eating is tricky, but it can be done. And it can be done with or without the kid knowing what you're doing.

Some youngsters love to be involved in making positive changes in the family. But others may find it stressful because they don't know how the changes will affect them. They may become upset when faced with an opportunity to vote on these changes, and their distress may lead to a power struggle with parents. The decision to include or exclude your kids from these food availability adjustments is up to you.

Ways to include your kids

If you think your kids will respond positively to your new ideas about eating, talk to them about what you've learned. Naturally, the information must be adjusted to the age of your kids. Keep it simple for little children, using sentences such as "It's important to always tell Mommy or Daddy when you get hungry." Older kids who can absorb more information may be more cooperative if they understand more specifically how body-controlled eating prevents weight and eating problems. (They can read sections of this book, if not the whole book. Otherwise, paraphrase the basic concepts for them.)

It may be valuable to discuss the Feast or Famine Cycle with preteens and teenagers, especially girls, because of their susceptibility to dieting at this age. Before they get trapped on the Feast or Famine Cycle, they can learn how to insulate themselves from it and save themselves from the nightmare of lifelong dieting. Preventing weight problems and eating struggles is much easier than trying to fix them after they become firmly established. Be sure your older kids understand that this is not a diet weight-loss program. If you suspect your kid already is dieting or has disturbed eating, try implementing the principles without any discussion, and see if things normalize. Basically, all kids should be taught to avoid going hungry, to eat on time, and to eat decent food. The following are the main points to cover when discussing your new eating approach with your kids:

1. Your body knows when you need fuel and tells you with hunger signals.
2. It's important always to eat when you get hungry.
3. Never, ever skip breakfast.
4. If you get hungry between meals, always eat good snacks or small meals.
5. If you get hungry at times during the day when you can't eat, tell me so we can plan better.
6. Pleasure foods (sweets and treats) are for special occasions, not for every day.

Show them or discuss the food lists so they learn what the higher quality foods are. This may be especially helpful for any kids who have already developed a weight problem. Food quality is crucial for them, but of course, avoiding famines is the bottom line. Teach younger children how to tell the difference between real food and poor-quality food. Then reinforce this information daily with your choices and comments.

Ten ways to involve your kids in quality body-controlled eating:

1. Ask your kids about their food preferences and respect all their opinions.
2. Ask your kids to help you make the grocery list, staying focused on the real foods.
3. Bring your kids to the grocery store to help buy plenty of real foods they like, both ready to eat and easy to prepare.
4. Invite your kids to dish up their meals buffet style— whatever amount of whatever foods they want.
5. Do not comment about your kids' eating, portions, or leftovers.
6. Do not argue if your kids say they are not hungry.
7. Do not argue if your kids say they are hungry.
8. Do not engage in power struggles over food. (Don't buy food you don't want your kids to eat.)
9. Do not become too rigid about food quality. This is a poor example.
10. Help your child or teen avoid going hungry by offering real food at regular intervals.

Changing the food supply

It all starts with adjusting the food availability—gradually usually works best. The first step is simple: Eliminate poor-quality foods slowly until they are gone or nearly so. Go through your cupboards, refrigerator, and freezer and list borderline and pleasure foods. If the list is short, good for you! You don't have far to go to achieve optimal food availability at home. But maybe your list is long and colorful. Take heart. You'll get there, too, in a few weeks. Now pick one or two of these poor-quality foods and throw them away. Yes, you heard me. Throw them in the garbage. They are not evil foods. They are simply not good enough for your kids' bodies. Remember, kids won't eat foods that are not there, and they won't be scrounging in the garbage can.

Your kids may miss these foods or beverages at first, but it's important to stand firm: "I know you are used to having Coke in the house, but it isn't really good for us to be drinking all the time. So, we'll stock your favorite drinks that are real food—juices, milk, sparkling water—just let me know what you want."

But what about food quality when your kids are away from home? Aren't they going to have Coke at the basketball games and at their friends' houses and even at school? Yes, they probably are—especially if they're used to having Coke. And, aside from encouraging them to drink beverages with some nutritional value, there's not much you can do about it. The part to focus on is the part you can control: Food that comes into your home.

It's a little easier to manage the food availability of a younger child, both at home and away. It's perfectly OK to ask a day-care provider to provide you with a list of snacks and meal foods offered to your kids. If they are decent, though imperfect, then relax. But if the quality falls extremely short, talk to the provider and tell her what you are trying to accomplish in your own home. Ask if you can help her improve the quality of the snacks and/or meals with her time and budget constraints in mind. And, of course, troubleshoot problems your individual child might be having in getting enough good food on time at a day-care center.

Schools have always had borderline menus, it seems. And now, with fast foods moving into many public high school cafeterias, most kids are eating high-fat fare almost daily during the school year. This is unfortunate, but it is not causing our country's rising rate of obesity and eating disorders among kids. Reckless undereating, delayed eating, going hungry, missing breakfast—these famines are the culprits behind weight and eating problems. The high-fat school lunches are make-up fat-storing food for kids who famine. And we can best protect our children by teaching them about the importance of body-controlled eating, and by helping them to stay tuned in to their hunger signals while controlling the food availability at home.

Once you've begun eliminating the first lower quality foods and once the protests (if there are any) are settling down, every few days, throw away another borderline/pleasure food that hasn't been eaten up. You can give it to the neighbors but it is better to get rid of it at once, rather than waiting to use it up. You don't want to use up cookies, ice cream, or coffee cake. You want it out of sight, out of mind, out of the house. But you're still not done with food availability. You know what your family is not going to eat, but what is there to eat?

Add an abundance of high-quality foods your kids like

Ask your kids what they like best for snacks and meals. You probably already know what they'll say, but it's good for them to think about their food preferences and tell you. Write down their favorites.

Some snacks and meal items will fall into the borderline/pleasure foods categories, but it is important not to criticize any food to your kids. This is betrayal. Instead, remind your kid that these foods are OK for special occasions but that you are trying to provide better quality food for everyday eating.

Solicit their help. Make suggestions. Keep their sweet or salty preferences in mind.

For example, kids who like dessert-type snacks and

pleasure desserts might like cinnamon-raisin toast with chocolate milk for a snack. Kids who prefer chips and salty foods may be happy with peanuts or almonds or cheese and crackers for snacks. Try to stay balanced. Your goal is to dramatically improve your kids' everyday food quality, not to make it rigidly perfect.

This doesn't mean your grocery list must be dictated by your kids' food preferences. It does mean you are respecting your kids' bodies and the food preferences those bodies have. Undoubtedly, our preferences for certain foods is linked to our physical need for those foods. Kids' bodies are no different.

Timmy is two years old and his brother Jeremy is almost four. A few weeks before his second birthday, Timmy woke up Jeremy at four o'clock in the morning, pulling him to the kitchen. The boys' mother heard them moving about and got up. She found Timmy pointing to the refrigerator, saying, "Peas... peas... peas." Jeremy said he didn't know what Timmy wanted and Timmy's mother thought the toddler was saying "please." Opening the refrigerator, Mom offered various foods: milk, juice, yogurt, cheese, bagels. Timmy shook his head to each. "Peas," he insisted. Finally it dawned on her. Timmy's mother took the leftover peas from the shelf and showed Timmy.

A big smile appeared across his face. "Peas!" he cried.

They all sat at the kitchen table and Timmy ate peas until he was done. Then his mother tucked him back into bed. This same scene occurred four nights in a row, and then the nighttime "Peascapade" ceased as mysteriously as it had begun.

Stock the real foods you know your kids like. Have these foods everywhere—on the countertop or ready to eat and reachable in the fridge or cupboard. Tape notes to cupboard doors or refrigerator, listing what is ready to eat inside.

Adjust your grocery list as you go along. Maybe you

were too idealistic at first, thinking your kids would go for raw veggies and dip after school. You discovered they wanted toast, bagels, or pizza instead. Simply adjust your shopping list and proceed. Gradually, this new eating style will become second nature for you and your kids too.

Offer food at typical hunger times
Breakfast

Always offer good foods your kids like for breakfast. In fact, institute a rule that no one leaves the house without something for breakfast, period. This means time must be allotted for this "most important meal of the day" every day.

It's best not to ask kids if they are hungry in the morning. They're sleepy. They may not know whether they're hungry or not. Or they may not feel like eating, even if they are hungry.

The best thing to do is to have food kids like ready for them to eat, whether they are three-years-old or fifteen. And it's important for kids to have enough time to eat what they need. Fifteen minutes less sleep given over to breakfast can make a big difference in the day. Some kids may not especially feel like eating right away when they get up, so having time to wake up for breakfast is important. They're certainly going to feel better an hour or two later when their bodies are happily burning through those quality calories. They'll be able to think straight and keep their cool under stress.

Kids who absolutely refuse breakfast should not be forced to eat. Offer light fare—toast, juice, cut-up fresh fruit. Don't fight about it. Some people seem to be born with a strong reluctance to eat right away. Do send portable snack food with these kids (e.g., granola bars, protein bars), so they can eat when they get hungry.

On the other hand, kids usually need substantial food for breakfast, and some breakfast foods are too light to hold them until lunch. This is a problem when kids don't have an opportunity to eat mid morning. Breakfasts that consist of mainly carbohydrates—cereal, breads, waffles and pancakes—are quickly digested and can leave kids hungry an hour or two later. (This is not a problem when kids can eat again, anytime.) Heavier breakfast foods such as eggs, ham, bacon, fried potatoes, and cheese will keep kids satisfied longer because they are digested more slowly and have more calories than lighter foods. This type of breakfast food is definitely a plus for kids in school all morning, so try to include heavier foods and protein in your kids' breakfasts. Include a slice of ham, some bacon, or cheese with their waffles. Add nuts to make granola cereals more substantial. Spread peanut butter or cream cheese on toast, bagels, or English muffins to increase calories, protein and fat. The fat in butter, peanut butter, cream cheese, breakfast meets, and eggs helps keep kids' hunger at bay until lunchtime.

Sometimes kids don't think about their hunger unless it's brought to their attention. Any time you know your kids have gone without food for a few hours, especially if they have been physically active, ask if they are hungry. Or simply put food in front of them. Many parents do this instinctively and it's a good thing. There's no worry about overfeeding a kid because kids who don't undereat don't overeat. Kids may also need help figuring out what they want or need to eat. Don't hover or worry about this. Simply making suggestions can help a hungry kid choose well. Here's an example:

Melanie bangs through the front door, letting her book bag drop with a thud. After a moment she slams the bathroom door.

"That you, Mel?" her dad inquires. After two and a half hours at soccer practice she is probably exhausted.

"Yeah, it's me. Who were you expecting, Santa Claus?" she says sarcastically.

"You sound hungry. How was practice?" Melanie

emerges from the bathroom.

"OK. I didn't play very well, and that Rhonda girl bugs me."

"Can I get you something? Make a pizza?"

"Yeah, I'm starved. I've been hungry since school let out. That didn't help either."

"I'll make a veggie pizza. That OK with you?"

"Thanks. Heavy on the cheese. I'll go shower."

After school

This is a very important time of day for kids' fuel needs. It is a rare child or teen who isn't hungry after school. Always have on hand good food that is ready to eat or easy to fix. Naturally, little children need supervision and help with snacks, but older kids often don't like to have to fuss around making something for themselves. Many would rather skip eating even though they are hungry. It isn't a high priority for them, especially for boys, I have observed. But ignoring this hungry time creates a famine, and the name of this game is famine avoidance. So how do parents make quality food ready to go for these kids? They plan ahead.

Sandwiches can be made ahead of time and refrigerated (peanut butter and jelly sandwiches don't need refrigeration). Homemade or canned soups can be heated in the microwave in two minutes. Cold cereal also makes a great snack. Fruits, vegetables, bagels, toast with toppings—all kinds of real foods can be ready to eat in no time after school, but they must be obviously available to kids and ready to eat or extremely easy to prepare.

Before sports, right after school

One of the most dangerous potential famine times happens when a sport or other physical activity is scheduled right after school. Kids who go right from the classroom to the gym or field often become hungry without a food source available. Here's why this time period is so dangerous:

High physical activity + hunger = severe famine.

Whether or not kids are hungry when they begin to use their bodies intensely, they often run out of fuel during the practice or work out. They may not feel hungry once their bodies get revved up—this is a natural adaptation—but they are in a famine, just the same. The evidence for this famine is in the postpractice intense hunger they feel when their bodies calm down.

Most adults have no idea this scenario is bad for kids' bodies because exercise has been touted as half the answer to obesity (the other half being to eat less, or eat low fat). But exercise without adequate quality food has the opposite effect: It actually sets up kids for weight problems and eating struggles because it is a famine. Famine-sensitive kids will adapt with symptoms of the Feast or Famine Cycle (and possibly weight gain and eating struggles). So, we see very active athletic fat kids and mystified parents, but the explanation is simply adaptation.

What can parents do for kids involved in after-school activities? They can and should provide portable food and drink for their kids to take with them when they leave home in the morning. These foods must "keep" in a backpack, so they need to be simple: granola bars, sports drinks, peanut butter and jelly sandwiches, cheese and crackers, fruit (fruit may not provide enough calories, depending on the kid and the activity), bagels and cream cheese, water. Make your own list tailored to your kid's preferences and appetite. Preventing a famine at this crucial time will not only protect your kid from weight and eating problems, it is certain to improve his or her performance as well.

A natural-born runner, Ryan signed up for cross-country as soon as it was offered in fifth grade. Practices were right after school so he worked out with the other runners for about an hour. With the returning bus ride, he got back home about an hour and a half later than he had before and complained to his mother of a headache. Ryan was used to eating right after school and didn't have anything to eat until after track.

It became apparent to his mother that Ryan needed to bring his after-school snack to school with him in the morning so he wouldn't run out of fuel and become hypoglycemic (low blood sugar). So Ryan packed his snack and ate it as soon as school let out. Running was much more fun when he wasn't starving, and he found he still needed a snack when he got home from practice!

Between meal snacks

Usually, three or four hours between meals is too long for body-controlled kids, especially little kids, to go without eating something. Most kids, with the exception of some adolescent boys, cannot take in enough calories at a meal to hold them until the next meal comes. So kids generally complain of hunger between meals. It is our job to see that they get quality food at these times to prevent a famine.

Traditional snack foods are small amounts of poor-quality food eaten on demand between meals, whereas meals are substantial amounts of food eaten at three fairly regular intervals. In order to keep our kids eating in a body-controlled way, tuned into their instincts, parents and caregivers must make high-quality snack foods available between breakfast and lunch and between lunch and supper. This high quality standard eliminates most common snacks, such as chips, cookies, Twinkies-like treats, cake, ice cream, brownies and candy bars. Although these foods have calories, which kids definitely need between meals, they don't have very high nutrient content—not like real foods. So look at the real foods list again and make your own list of snacks your kids like. Always keep these on hand.

An hour before a meal is ready

This is a maddening time for adults who are preparing or picking up a wholesome meal. "I'm hungry!" a kid complains. It seems like precious little to ask that the kid simply wait the half hour, hour, or ninety minutes. But for kids, that time span is far too long to go hungry. So there's only one thing to do. Get some quality food into them to prevent a famine, but not too much fuel or they will miss the upcoming meal because they are too full. Sometimes fruit or vegetable juices or bite-sized fruit/vegetable pieces work well for these little urgencies. But if kids insist on something more substantial, try something like cheese or peanut butter on crackers.

      With adolescents, this is more complicated. For example, Rob, sixteen, complains that he is starving after football practice, and it's an hour before Dad picks up supper from the local Chinese take-out. Rob insists on having pizza when he gets home. Fine. He is really hungry. Let him fix a small pizza and remind him that the Chinese food is coming in an hour. He'll most likely still be hungry when it arrives. If not, he can eat the take-out leftovers later. If mealtime is a family affair, and a kid has eaten in advance because of this type of situation, have him sit with the family even if he is not eating. All family members eating at the same time is not as important as being together.

Tips and suggestions for food quality control at home and away

At home

Controlling the food availability at home is extremely simple as long as the adults are the only ones bringing in food and they are all committed to high-quality eating. Such a commitment means that you generally don't purchase or bring into your home foods that are poor quality, including borderline and pleasure foods. Of course there are exceptions! Birthday cakes and special-occasion pleasure foods are perfectly fine. But special occasions do not happen three or four times a week. If they do, they are not special. They are simply occasions for poor-quality eating. Here are some tips for at-home quality control:

1. Eat well, yourself, before you grocery shop.
2. Stick to your grocery list of high-quality foods that the kids (and adults) like.
3. To avoid buying low-class foods on impulse, avoid eye contact with them.
4. Shop for groceries twice a week instead of once to maintain fresh supplies. Two quick trips are some times easier than one big one.
5. Listen to your kids when they tell you what they like and don't like. This may change from week to week.
6. If your kids don't eat the quality foods you stock, ask why. Make adjustments.
7. Once a special occasion has passed, dispatch left over pleasure foods to the garbage. Yes you can.
8. When you are given gifts of borderline or pleasure foods, graciously accept them, enjoy for a day or two, then throw or give the rest away.

Away from home

It is more difficult to control the food quality of your kids' diets away from home. Obviously, you are not there to oversee it. But there are some things you can do to improve the quality of their diet when they are at school, at a neighbor's house, at sports practice, and with other supervising adults away from home.

1. Remind kids—and help them, if necessary—to prepare high-class food to take along when they leave home if it won't be available where they are going.
2. Discuss the food choices kids have at school and other places they frequent. Encourage the better choices that they like.
3. Ask your kids when they get hungry in the morning at school, and find out if their teacher is open to quality snacks in the classroom.
4. If there is a "no food outside the cafeteria" policy at your kids' school and your kids become very hungry more than an hour before lunch, arrange for them to get a snack break in the morning (for "medical reasons" if necessary). Send appropriate food along for that snack
5. For younger kids, inform parents supervising overnights that your kids need to eat whenever they are hungry but you prefer meal-type foods to typical snacks. Send some along for the group.

Of course, you can't totally control the food your child or teenager eats when away from home, so don't try. Realistic efforts in more manageable areas will make a big difference in your child's overall diet and eating habits. Always remember, preventing famines is crucial, particularly the undereating, delayed eating and going-hungry types of famines because they set up a kid's body for the worst trouble. In fact, even if the food quality of our kids' diets is excellent, if they go hungry regularly, they are vulnerable to weight problems and/or disturbed eating patterns.

Finicky eaters

Although he was always a finicky eater from birth, my son Joe insisted on an extremely limited diet for a period of about two years when he was between eight and ten. My other children were never as picky as Joe. During those two years, he was willing to eat only these foods: cold cereal, milk, spaghetti (no meat or chunks), grilled cheese sandwiches (American cheese only on white bread), oriental stir-fry (no cauliflower, no peppers, no celery, no mushrooms, no pea pods, no water-cress), white rice, cheese pizza, McDonald's hamburgers, and french fries. Oh, and Dairy Queen ice cream cones—plain.

Joe was adamant about his taste buds. When he smelled new foods or foods he said he didn't like he'd grimace and pull away as if sniffing ammonia. Obviously, this wasn't simply a power struggle.

The good news is, Joe grew and developed in a per-fectly normal way in spite of his self-restricted diet. He was always at least average in height and weight until he began body-building as a teen. Then he added protein drinks to his diet and his weight increased as his muscles developed. Now his friends call him "the Beast." He's twenty-one and still has strong food preferences, although he seems to be trying dif-ferent dishes more often.

When kids are in the throes of the finicky years, it can drive parents crazy and worry them too. How are these finicky eaters ever going to grow up healthy and strong? In the same way that almost all toddlers become potty trained before kindergarten, almost all kids learn to eat a variety of nutritious food by adulthood. It helps to understand that picky eating is usually limited to a few months or years, and that kids snap out of it just as mysteriously as it appeared.

The best way to deal day-to-day with this problem is to keep offering a balanced variety of good foods to all kids. Those too young to prepare food for themselves may require short-order service when they refuse food prepared for the family. Minimize these times by always serving food the finicky eater prefers in addition to the family meal. Once kids can fix quality food for themselves, they should have the option of substituting a preferred food for ones they refuse.

If you are alarmed at your kid's finicky eating habits, see your pediatrician. Write down specifically what and when your child is eating for three days before the appointment. You may need additional guidance, reassurance, or both.

Adolescents with minds of their own

As you read about managing the food availability of teenagers, you might be thinking, there is nothing I can do with my teens. They eat their own peculiar way and there is no influencing them. How can I possibly affect their eating habits? Carefully, that's how.

Because teenagers, and especially girls, are so vulnerable to eating disorders and unhealthy eating patterns, it is extremely important that adults gingerly address the issue of diet and eating behavior. Actually, it's best if you solicit information from your teen before offering any information or advice. Find out where she is with her diet—whether she cares much or is courting an eating struggle. Reassure her that your interest in her diet is simply that you want to make sure she is getting enough decent food often enough to be healthy and energetic. It's usually less threatening to kids, especially sensitive teens, if you talk in terms of improving the whole family's food quality and availability. We'll talk more later about "The Do It Yourself" approach.

Although parents can teach any age kid that it's important to listen to your body and always eat when you are hungry, there's a big advantage in training older kids. You can explain to them the principles of *why* it is so important to stay tuned in to their bodies. You can teach them about their unique adaptive potential and their individual famine sensitivity. You can tell them about the symptoms of the Feast or Famine Cycle to make them more aware of their own bodies' signals of distress. When teenagers really get ahold of this information, as my daughter Genevieve did when she was thirteen, they can set sail for a lifetime free of weight and eating troubles.

But what if your adolescents totally resist this information? Not to worry. The changes you make in the food availability at home will set a new standard for food quality, and this will certainly affect their eating at home. And your own eating choices will be demonstrating what the better quality foods are. Kids usually learn more from example than indoctrination. Don't wage a war. It's not worth it and you will lose. Simply make the changes you know are good for your family, and everyone's eating will improve as the food improves.

If your kids vehemently resist changing the quality of food in their diet, then there is one message they may still be able to hear: Eat on time. Understanding the importance of eating on time is the most basic and crucial if kids are going to remain body-controlled eaters. Delayed eating and then doing poor-quality make-up eating is rampant among our children and teens, and this is the crux of their rising obesity rate. If we can simply get them to tune into their hunger signals and eat food every time their bodies request fuel, we will have conquered much of the weight struggles we have among our kids.

The top priority is getting kids to eat on time.
Then improve food quality whenever possible.

Eight ways to encourage children and teens to eat on time

1. Make sure there is enough time for kids to eat as much as they want in the morning, every morning.
2. Make sure plenty of real foods that kids like are available for breakfast.
3. Troubleshoot mid-morning hunger times by making sure quality food they like is available then.
4. Interrupt smaller kids at play two hours after meals and offer them real-food snacks and drinks.
5. After school, whether at home or away, offer all school-age children real food they like.

6. If you know your kids haven't eaten for a while, ask them if they are hungry or thirsty. If they are, feed them real food or drinks.
7. Send quality snacks and beverages with kids who have sports practice or other activities after school.
8. Provide high-quality foods for lunch and supper at regular times.

Here's a little something for your refrigerator. The commandments are for everyone: your kids, your spouse, and you.

Ten Commandments for body-controlled eating

I. I am your one and only body. Feed me well whenever I get hungry.

II. Remember to keep plenty of high-quality real food on hand at all times.

III. You shall not buy pleasure or borderline foods on a regular basis.

IV. Honor your hunger and other body-need signals.

V. You shall not delay eating.

VI. You shall not go hungry.

VII. You shall prepare for hunger needs while away from home.

VIII. You shall not eat low-class foods on a regular basis.

IX. You shall choose the best foods possible when visiting restaurants and relatives.

X. You shall support body-controlled eating in others.

Exercise

Where does exercise fit into all this? It's no panacea against kids' weight problems. Young, overweight athletes are common. But there seems to be a correlation between lack of exercise and childhood/teen obesity, and there is. But it's not what we have been taught.

The prevailing attitude is that kids don't exercise enough and that's why they get fat. This is only partially true. The part that's missing is *why* kids' bodies continue to take in more calories than they are burning up, and *why* they don't exercise.

Kids who go hungry on a regular basis and are famine sensitive experience all five adaptive responses—increased appetite, decreased metabolic rate, cravings for fat-producing foods, preoccupation with food and avoidance of physical activity. The first, third, and fourth adaptations account for why these overweight kids continue to eat more food than their bodies are using up. When kids don't eat enough good food when they need it, their bodies must have extra calories to store food for emergency fuel. Increased appetite, cravings and preoccupation are all about increasing caloric intake. The decrease in metabolic rate and avoidance of physical activity are about conserving calorie expenditure. So kids' bodies react to famines by taking more in and burning less. Makes sense, doesn't it?

In light of these adaptive responses, it doesn't make sense to try to get overweight kids, who all famine regularly, to exercise more. In fact, this tactic just makes their famines more severe and most likely leads to more weight gain. Many kids who have tried this approach only get heavier and more discouraged.

On the other hand, kids who eat plenty of real food whenever they are hungry—body-controlled eaters—are inclined to be active. Kids have a natural physical restlessness (that seems to wane in adulthood) and they need the food to fuel it. Of course, like their unique personalities, there are differences among kids—extremes of activity level, from hyperactive to calm and sedentary. But wherever kids fall on this spectrum, they need enough quality food to be energetic at all times of the day.

There are other reasons for kids' inactivity. Kids who

are cooped up inside without the chance to be physically active are obviously more sedentary. So kids of all ages need opportunities to move around throughout the day, whether at school or at home. As teachers know, kids become restless and lose their concentration after a period of sitting. Children should be allowed time to stretch during any class that lasts for more than 30 minutes. Teenagers can go longer without a break but also benefit from occasional two-minute stretches during class.

Recess is not nearly as popular as it once was. This should change. Group games, rope jumping, hop scotch, foot racing, tug of war, king of the hill, and many other favorites provide benefits of vigorous exercise for kids. They also allow kids an opportunity to learn social skills and build stronger character. Schools must recognize the undeniable benefits that recess periods provide and make recess a priority once again for kids' sake.

The school day is not the only time kids need breaks. Kids on the computer, kids watching TV, and kids doing homework, all need to be reminded to take breaks and have some physical fun. Here's an example:

"You've been writing that paper for more than two hours," Trevor's mother says, leaning into the computer room.

"Yeah, I know. It's due tomorrow and I'm only half done," Trevor says.

"Why don't you go out and shoot some hoops for a while. You'll probably be able to work faster after a break."

"I don't know." Trevor hesitates. "Well, I guess I will. I'm not concentrating that great anymore."

Encourage your kids to run around, go outside, rake leaves, weed the garden, sweep the walkway, climb a tree, ride a bike, shoot hoops, practice soccer, play tennis, go golfing, go fishing, throw a ball, do cartwheels, make snowmen, go ice skating, go swimming, do something.

Invest in a ping-pong table, a basketball hoop, or a

foosball table. Make physical games and activities a higher priority when selecting holiday gifts.

Don't be timid about limiting TV watching and computer time. Sit down with your kids and tell them that there are limits on these privileges. Together work out the times and programs they want to watch on TV and how much they can play games on the computer. Don't allow your kids to "accidentally" engage in these activities. Instead, select specific shows to watch and games to play, on purpose—based on your decisions. This kind of scheduling will limit these sedentary activities and allow for more active play and recreation.

A boy from a nearby junior high school came to my door, fundraising for his school. His mother waited in the car in the street about ten yards away. Our neighborhood is tightly packed with small houses. It was sunny and warm outside, and we enjoy a very safe neighborhood. The boy walked from my door to the car, got in, and rode to the next house, about fifty feet away. Then they drove to the next house, and to the next.

Whenever possible, let your kids walk wherever they want or need to go. I remember my son, Joe, asking me to drive him three blocks to his friend's house. Just say no. Kids need to walk and run more, and parents must stop coddling them.

If you need ideas for inside and outside physical activities for kids of various ages, consult the Internet, a library or bookstore. Be creative and practical. Kids don't have to be doing jumping jacks to be getting exercise. Focus on finding opportunities for kids to move around more—any kind of moving—and you'll be improving their health and teaching them valuable lifelong lessons.

The do-it-yourself approach applies here as well as to our eating behavior. Kids are all influenced by their parents' lifestyle and commitment to physical activity. Do you take walks regularly? Do you play yard or beach/water sports? Do you enjoy sports and active hobbies or belong to a team or league? Do you work out at home or at a club? How much TV do you watch? Most of us have room to improve.

So far, we've covered teaching better food quality, important guidelines about eating behavior, and being active lifestyle models. But if we want to keep kids from the struggles of obesity and eating disorders, we must focus even more on positive role modeling. We must become good examples to our kids. They naturally identify with us and want to be like us, and we must use this principle to train them to be body-controlled eaters and physically active. We can use this identification principle to help solidify healthy eating patterns and physical activity in our kids, and there's only one way to do it: We have to do it ourselves.

Take the Do-It-Yourself Approach

8

Teach your kids instinctive eating by practicing it with them.

We know the problems of obesity and eating disorders in children are growing, but now we also know how reckless eating patterns contribute to these problems. And we know that we can correct these unhealthy patterns in our kids. But can you get your kids to eat right while you continue in the old careless eating patterns yourself? Not likely.

So get ready to apply all the principles of body-controlled eating to yourself, your spouse and anyone else in the household. It's the only way to successfully indoctrinate your kids in this program and prevent eating problems for life. If you already have a weight problems or eating struggle, you'll be able to interrupt the Feast or Famine Cycle that has caused your adaptive symptoms. If you are already a body-controlled eater, you have a head start, but keep reading. You may learn some things along the way.

Changing eating patterns is difficult—for individuals as well as families. It's clear by now that the *Naturally Thin*

Kids approach necessarily requires changes for the whole family—including every child, teen, and adult living together. In many ways, this makes it easier. There's support built in. It can become a crusade or project in a family. The whole crew can get involved. But parents must choose whether to lead by example or not.

Parents or caregivers who apply the principles of body-controlled eating to their own eating behavior can more successfully support instinctive eating in children and adolescents in their households.

Kids tend to do what we do, more than what we tell them to do. Parents whose diets are high quality and whose eating is body controlled tend to teach and support instinctive eating in their kids by example. They take their kids' hunger seriously because it would never occur to them to unnecessarily tolerate going hungry themselves. Hunger is not a threat to these naturally thin people. It is a sign that fuel is needed, and they instinctively seek it out, just as little kids naturally do. Fortunately, they have escaped the tangle of theories and half-truths about food and eating that our culture is inundated with, and they tend to pass along this natural freedom to their children. What a valuable legacy!

But many parents and kids' caregivers eat recklessly, skipping meals, eating poor quality food as daily fare. Or as dieters, they have tried to intellectually control, one way or another, what and when and how much they have eaten—for years, sometimes for decades. The changeover for these adults can be difficult, even quite stressful. But it is important enough to struggle through to the other side. There's a lot at stake for everyone, kids and adults alike.

Is it necessary for parents to be body-controlled eaters to support it in their kids?

It's possible for kids' caregivers to feed their children according to the children's eating instincts while ignoring their own body signals. But it is far better for adults who care for kids to practice instinctive eating right along with their charges. There are several important reason this is true:

1. Kids learn by watching adult behavior and choices.
2. Kids tend to imitate what parents and other adults do.
3. One set of rules for eating in a group is far simpler to follow than two or three.
4. Consistency in kids' and adults' eating behaviors reinforces the principles of body-controlled eating for both groups.
5. The principles of healthful eating do not change with age.

The path to body-controlled eating for adults is exactly the same as the one for kids, except that adults are usually in charge of their own food supply. Tuning in to your hunger signals and always eating quality food whenever you are hungry is the rule of thumb for adults, too.

Preparing for your own hungry times away from home will help remind you of your kids' fuel needs away from home. Noticing that you get hungry at odd times and in the middle of things, such as shopping, will remind you that eating by instinct is sometimes erratic, just as your kids' appetites are. As you apply the Naturally Thin principles and get used to eating on time, you may not tolerate going hungry very well. This might happen to your kids too, if they have been used to famines and instinctive eating is a big change.

The Do-It-Yourself Approach

There are three subgroups of all kids' caretakers. Find yourself in one of them:

1. adults who are already instinctive, body-controlled eaters

2. adults who often eat recklessly by accident because life interferes with eating properly
3. adults who diet (restrict eating on purpose) much of the time and experience the symptoms of the Feast or Famine Cycle.

Adults who do it naturally

For parents and caregivers who are already essentially body-controlled eaters, the adjustment is usually a snap. But almost all adults can improve the food availability in their lives, even those who are already eating instinctively much of the time.

It may be easier for these adults to understand and consistently apply the principles of body-controlled eating because they have always heeded their body's eating instincts. They probably don't suffer from weight or eating struggles, certainly not serious ones. And these adults will find it easier to teach their kids because they'll be teaching something they know from experience.

Reckless adult eaters

This category probably contains the largest number of people. Most Americans eat regularly in haste, eat on the run, eat lousy food, miss meals, tolerate excessive hunger and overeat. Our reckless diets result from many factors, some of which we've discussed: hectic schedules, poor prioritizing, inadequate food supply, insufficient time, and lack of knowledge.

Adults who eat in the typical reckless American way will need to seriously adjust their habits in order to integrate the Naturally Thin principles into their own and their kids' lives. This will require substantial discipline and effort for the first few months especially. But these grown-ups stand to benefit in the same way as their kids. They'll feel better, have more energy, and enjoy normal appetites. If they are over-weight from their reckless eating, they'll gradually lose weight.

Parents and caregivers who have been dieters

If you've been a dieter for some time, taking this Naturally Thin approach, yourself, may seem daunting, but you can do it. You'll probably especially crave sweets and/or fatty foods, but you're going to stop dieting (mind-controlled eating) and start eating instinctively (body-controlled eating). And gradually, as you stop going hungry, these cravings (adaptive symptoms of the Feast or Famine Cycle), will go away. This is a good sign that your body is finally being satisfied with decent food when you need it.

   If you have recently lost weight by dieting, especially if you lost it quickly, you will probably gain weight when you introduce body-controlled eating. The undereating program or diet that you followed to lose weight was a famine to your body. It trained your body to need to store fat for upcoming famines in the future.

   Once you let go of the mind control over your eating, your body will take over, adjust your appetite upward, keep your metabolism down, and accumulate fat for survival insurance. There's nothing you can do about it, so you may as well enjoy it. Sooner or later, statistics show, you'll gain back the weight anyway. Once your body's physiological need for fat is satisfied, you will level off. *It is imperative to stay with good-quality, high-nutrient food and always eat on time.* Remember, you're developing habits that will serve you well for two life-times—yours and your kids'.

Ready, set, eat!

Converting to body-controlled eating isn't as tough as most parents and caregivers think. But where do you start? All adults who want to have naturally thin kids will have to apply the Do It Yourself Approach by beginning in the same place you start for kids—with food availability. While you're shopping with their real food needs in mind, list yours as well. Leave the low-class borderline and pleasure foods in the grocery store. The changes you'll focus on first are *the type of foods you bring into your household, including quality and variety.* Next, look at the quality of food you choose away from home. Usually, we can make big improvements there. And yes, you can eat high-quality foods with your taste buds in mind.

Once you establish a body-controlled eating lifestyle, the rewards, for both you and your kids, become obvious:

1. You will all feel better.
2. You will have more energy with regular quality fuel to burn.
3. Your moods will probably be more stable, without intermittent blood-sugar crises throughout the day.
4. You will gradually lose cravings for sweet and fatty foods, or they will become much less intense.
5. The tendency to overeat, especially at night, will decrease, and you will be able to decide not to eat at night even if you are a little hungry.
6. Eating from boredom, stress, or anxiety will disappear too.

These changes all reflect ending the Feast or Famine Cycle and once you eliminate the famines that perpetuate the cycle, the cycle ends and all the adaptive symptoms end with it.

Eating after the supper meal is almost always a symptom of the cycle because night eating before bedtime is the best time for bodies to use the calories consumed for fat production. Daytime undereaters tend to eat and overeat later in the day as a direct result of going hungry or undereating earlier. But once bodies get sufficient calories and nutrients throughout the day and the famine stress is eliminated, nighttime eating wanes dramatically. And those who want to lose weight can choose to avoid eating at this time and go to bed empty rather than full. This gives bodies a chance to burn excess fuel that is now unnecessary.

What are we up against?

In our attempt to support our kids in body-controlled eating and perhaps rediscover our own eating instincts, we are up against a diet-obsessed culture that actually promotes undereating and going hungry. Our society does not recognize that going hungry, delayed eating and undereating actually cause and accelerate the development of weight and eating problems.

Talking to hundreds of overweight adults and kids has convinced me that undereating drives the Feast or Famine Cycle, the wheel of adaptation responsible for excess weight gain. The solution to excess weight that we have been touting in the U.S. for more than fifty years is "eat less, exercise more." And where has this "remedy" gotten us? It has made us fatter—at an alarming rate.

Reckless eating by itself (which includes delayed eating and eating poor-quality food), promotes weight gain in famine-sensitive people, but not usually serious excess weight unless there is extreme famine sensitivity. It takes the mind-controlled eating of the traditional diet to cause serious adaptive obesity. I have never met an obese person, adult or kid, who had not tried to lose weight by seriously restricting their food intake, both by conscious and unconscious food avoidance.

This is the fatal irony: **We are trying to fix a serious, life-and joy-threatening disorder *with its most basic cause.*** And researchers are mystified even though they keep making new discoveries about ways human bodies adjust to undersatisfied hunger. For example, they have identified a number of biochemicals that are produced in response to famines. One is called lipoprotein lipase. This enzyme is thought to be responsible for the rebound weight gain that dieters almost always experience.

But, instead of considering why this enzyme is elevated in dieters, and what it is about how dieters eat that stimulates the production of this fat-promoting chemical, scientists try to develop a pill that will neutralize this enzyme. The only way to avoid the production of lipoprotein lipase is body-controlled eating, and avoiding famine, the stimulus for its production.

Are we so far gone in our lack of respect for the profound and delicate workings of our bodies? Haven't we already discovered with fen-phen and many other diet "breakthroughs" that undereating does not fix obesity in the long run and can even cause serious damage?

The "eat less, control your appetite" diet mindset of our culture nags relentlessly at us. It's easy to slip back into frequent famines, both quantitative and qualitative. It's a familiar pattern—more familiar than instinctive eating—and easier too. How does a family keep on the path? For those who have wandered far off, it may be very challenging, especially for the first few months.

The Path

Our culture has already cut a wide path to obesity and eating disorders by

- massively promoting artificial eating controls
- not prioritizing quality food availability
- disseminating confusing and contradictory diet misinformation
- touting short-sighted quick-fix diets known to fail more than 95 percent of the time.

Real fat weight cannot be lost quickly and permanently. It isn't possible. Yet the propaganda goes on and on and on as dieters become fatter and fatter, and more and more people become dieters. We, as a country, are on this wide path, and it is leading us into an epidemic of obesity and eating disorders.

The path to a family's natural, instinctive eating behavior is necessarily narrow. We must stand against a strong current, one you may not have thought about before. For example, eating on time in our society is very inconvenient for most people. As soon as you try to apply this principle for yourself or for your kids, you will discover this. In spite of the fact that we are a society with food all around—on every street corner—you will be challenged to have quality food on hand whenever and wherever you get hungry, and to arrange for your kids to have it, too.

You will get caught in traffic, hungry, with nothing decent in the car to eat. You will find yourself at your desk at work, mid morning, with a growling stomach and no food available until lunch. You will find yourself rushing around in the morning, hungry for breakfast but without the time to eat a quality meal. You will discover that every day at 4:00 you are very hungry (though you never noticed before) and you have nothing to eat at that odd hour as you drive your kids to lessons or practice or finish up your last hour of work.

All around you you'll see the eat-less diet message—in television commercials, in magazines, on the Internet, in junk mail ads. It's enough to make you feel crazy. Here you are, trying to learn how to eat, and the diet propaganda out there is offering a completely revolutionary breakthrough way for you to avoid eating. If avoiding eating by restricting calories and drinking calorie-free drinks when you are hungry really worked, all the dieters in the land (and there are millions) would be happily model-thin by now.

Teaching kids to notice unhealthy messages

Children and adolescents need a vaccine against the crazy and often contradictory messages our culture sends about eating and food. They need to be taught to notice what traditional eat-less diet propaganda says and to understand why it is so harmful. There is no one in the world better suited to inoculate them through education than their parents.

So it is up to you. If you are trying to lose weight by controlling your food intake (limiting calories, skipping meals, and avoiding food), your children are much more likely to see this as reasonable behavior, no matter what you tell them to do. TV and magazine ads for products that promote rapid weight loss through appetite suppression will seem perfectly rational to them. To ensure your child's immunity to weight problems and eating struggles, you must take a stand against popular beliefs about weight control and eating, and venture out in faith—faith in your kid's body, faith in the great Designer of our bodies.

If we are going to make our kids aware of the potential dangers of this crazy diet culture we live in, we must heighten our own awareness.

- Pay attention to all the quick weight loss, eat-less messages coming at you from the media.
- Notice the unrealistic thinness of models and movie stars.
- Note the television commercials for quick-weight-loss products, including the ever-popular meal replacement drinks.
- Look at the magazine racks at grocery check-out lanes and count the number of articles on how to lose weight—tips and tricks in every single edition.

We are positively inundated with this take-off-five-pounds-overnight thinking, and it is making us fatter as a nation. We must start seeing it for what it is—dangerous propaganda that leads ultimately to weight gain and eating problems—if we want to steer our kids clear of its destruction in their lives.

Once we adults identify the misinformation our culture is feeding us, we can caution our kids about it. We can discuss with them the messages about dieting and quick weight loss. We can educate them about diet commercials, reassuring them that their bodies know how to stay slim if they will keep listening to their bodies instead of TV and keep eating good food whenever they get hungry.

In our culture, kids at earlier and earlier ages begin to worry about their bodies being OK. So they need more reassurance than ever that they have good bodies and they don't have to worry about getting fat. Again, this message is most effective when adults in the child's life are eating instinctively and aren't worried about their own bodies.

Because our culture is preoccupied with thinness and beauty, our kids get the message very early that these things are very important. Sometimes kids as young as six and seven are already worried about their body shape and size and attractiveness. This is tragic. With so many worthwhile things for kids to focus on during childhood and adolescence, their physical features should not compete for their attention. But that's what happens, and kids need help from the adults in their lives to feel good about their bodies, imperfections and all.

For more information on how you can appy the Naturally Thin principles to your own eating patterns, check the author's website: www.naturally-thin.com

Reshape Body Image Standards

9

Reprogramming your kids' positive body image is essential.

The future of our children is at stake. Obesity carries with it a social stigma that is worse, in ways, than many other handicaps. This is true for children as well as adults. Overweight kids suffer discrimination, prejudice, social rejection, ridicule, and even physical attacks because of their excess weight. Less inhibited and more impulsive and honest about their feelings, kids lash out recklessly at other kids who don't measure up to their ideas of "normal."

Rejection and ridicule always affect a child's personality, which must adapt to this hostility. Overweight kids may develop all sorts of coping mechanisms to get through this abuse, and these coping skills and defenses linger throughout life for many. Burdened with this "sin that shows," fat kids often do not experience the relatively carefree time that childhood is supposed to be.

Whether or not parents are concerned about potential weight problems and eating disorders in their kids specifically,

163

all parents want their kids to feel good about their bodies. It's part of healthy self-esteem. I call it body esteem. But relatively few kids have what they consider ideal bodies, and fewer and fewer are happy with their bodies as they grow through the teenage years. By the time young women go to college, more than 75 percent are unhappy with their shape and/or weight while only about 20 percent are actually overweight.

Boys are not usually as vocal about their discontent, but if you pry a bit, they'll confide their own style of body rejection: shoulders too small, legs too short, undertall, over-weight, bad hair, ears stick out. Our culture doesn't lend itself to contentment in this area.

Why are we overly concerned with beauty and body shape and size? And, more importantly, how can we protect our kids and teens from this plague of anxiety about physical imperfection? If we can help kids feel happier with whatever their body shape is and if we can help them accept other kids' imperfect bodies, then we've accomplished a lot.

How to program your kids' positive body image

We all have physical imperfections and so do our kids. Even supermodels have them. That's why their photographs are retouched! These imperfections themselves are not the prob-lem, then, because they are universal. It is our attitudes and our beliefs about our bodies' negative attributes that make them significant to us.

These attitudes and beliefs are *acquired or learned.* So adults can play a vital role in their kids' body image. Kids develop their body self-image *first* from the adults in their lives. What we as parents say about our own bodies and espe-cially the things we say about our children's bodies influence kids' attitudes and beliefs about their own physiques.

How can you positively influence your kids' body image and general self-esteem? Develop good relationships with your kids in all areas. If the platform of love and acceptance isn't there, it isn't likely that your kids, particularly in their teen years, will listen to your opinions, much less accept your support. Affirming body image is only a small part of your whole relationship, but it is an increasingly important one in warding off the nightmare of lifelong weight and eating struggles.

Affirm your kids' strengths

Notice positive attributes about your kids in everyday situations. The most important qualities to comment about concern the person he or she is—character, personality, natural talents, and uniqueness. Regularly complimenting them in these areas supports your kids' sense of themselves, their core identity as a unique and worthwhile person.

Don't exaggerate. Don't flatter. Never be insincere. But every single person has characteristics worthy of a sincere compliment.

A thirteen-year-old daughter delights in wearing wildly colorful, exotic-looking punk clothes. Her mom stands at the door as Daughter leaves to catch the bus. "You are very creative in putting your outfits together," Mom says with a quick hug. Comments like these, of course, must be delivered with love and sincerity or they may be misinterpreted as sarcasm.

Sometimes it's a matter of noticing little things. A dad sees his son hurrying to get to practice on time. "I admire the commitment you've made to hockey this year," he says.

Psychologists say that parents reinforce the behaviors they notice the most, whether good or bad. Take care to catch your kids doing the right thing, making the right choice, working hard, trying. And encourage them in it.

Sometimes we can draw out our kids' true feelings by listening and asking follow-up questions. "You are very graceful when you do your dance routine," a father tells his little daughter after dance class.

"The other girls are better than me," she mumbles. This signals a need for reassurance, so don't miss comments like these. Take them seriously.

Dad replies, "I don't think the other girls are better. What makes you think so?" This exchange has opened an opportunity for this dad to meet his child's need, which is part of a healthy parent-child relationship.

Sometimes we have to back up and look at our kids more objectively to really appreciate them. After two hours of helping with math homework, a frustrated mother sighs, "I see your determination in math," she says, "and I'm proud of you."

Character counts, too. So let your kid know you notice. "I heard about how kind you were to the new boy in school today," Mom says. "That's so important."

Communicating appreciation is a skill we can develop and use every day. Whenever they help us, for example, we can encourage our kids by simply saying, "It's great to know I can count on your help when I need it."

One of the chief distinctions between adults and kids is that kids play more. They can bring us out of our more serious preoccupations and help us to "be in the now" more often. We might tell them, "I enjoy your sense of humor," and laugh with them often.

Or we might say, "Your loyalty to your friends is very impressive." Maybe we don't even like her friends. Perhaps there have been fights about clothes, hanging out, smoking. But one thing is sure: Your daughter is loyal to her friends, and that truly is amazing!

Remember when your baby learned the game "How big is baby? Soooooooo big!"? Do you recall how big your baby actually was at that time? Not too big. Most babies learn that game before they are even toddlers. But they throw their arms up with the cue, How big is baby? and make themselves as tall as their chubby little arms will extend.

Highly suggestible, babies grow into older kids who never really lose some of that openness to their parents' affirmations.

Make a list of your kids' strengths and keep it somewhere handy. Add to the list when you notice new assets and review it occasionally to remind yourself to commend your kid for these strengths. Children and teens who are affirmed for positive qualities that have nothing to do with their appearance are less likely to rely too much on their physical features for their self-esteem.

But what about their physical features? Should you just ignore kids' bodies altogether?

Affirm your kids' physical strengths, including body features

It's unrealistic and unnecessary to ignore kids' bodies in an attempt to protect them from preoccupation with their appearance. In fact, it could backfire. It's better for adults to maintain a balanced attitude about appearance: It's important to look nice for others but looks aren't everything. Strive to give kids confidence about how they look and a relaxed attitude about their overall appearance. With an "I am OK" and "I look OK" attitude, kids can get on with the important things about being kids and growing up.

To an adolescent in an awkward stage of growth, pointing out even one positive feature can boost a sagging ego. Elaina's mom remarks, "You have especially pretty hair," giving a much-needed lift to an insecure teen.

"I like the way you stand so tall," or "Your shoulders are getting broad" or "You are growing more beautiful/handsome every day," are all comments that may help kids develop confidence about their appearance. But these comments must be made sincerely and in a routine way if they are to supply the platform for kids' confidence in their appearance, one part of healthy overall self-esteem.

Won't kids get the wrong message with their parents always telling them how good they look? No. First of all, we aren't going to be telling kids how good they look all the time. Parents can comment about appearance occasionally when they notice a body or facial feature they can compliment in a nonchalant, matter-of-fact way. Kids need positive feedback from their parents about their looks so they can relax and feel confident about that part of their life. Then kids are less likely to be oversensitive to criticism from others. They'll also be less likely to take their appearance too seriously, while neglecting more important areas of development.

This type of support is a bit tricky because it's possible to overdo it. But kids who grow up in a positive environment where their bodies are viewed as acceptable (though imperfect) are more likely to enjoy freedom from the physical self-rejection rampant in our culture.

We have to counter society's strong negative messages about thinness, perfection, sexiness, and macho bodies. With occasional positive comments, we can help free our kids to be themselves and to enjoy and take care of their bodies.

Avoid making any derogatory comments about your kid's physical appearance

Kids are in the experimental stage of life. From their first hours out of the womb, they are trying things out. Our responses to their experimentations can powerfully influence them. This is how children are socialized. When we aren't paying attention to the big picture, however, careless reactions can actually *discourage* aspects of their personalities we want to encourage.

Parents and kids often get into power struggles over clothing, hairstyles, and makeup—all kinds of choices kids make about adorning themselves. But when offering guidance, insisting on refinements, we need to respect our kids and their choices. At times kids, even more than adults, are trying to say something about themselves in these choices and the wise parent looks and listens for the message behind the choice.

For example, at age eleven, Rick was muscular and athletic but still had the padding of childhood while his friends were lean and taller than he. His mother knew he was very self-conscious about his body. He began to choose baggy, oversized clothes (before they were popular). He told his mother they were more comfortable, but she knew he felt better with his body size obscured by a lot of extra material.

Although Rick's mom thought the big clothes actually accentuated Rick's extra weight, she complimented him on his choice of style and color and made no negative remarks about either his weight or his oversized clothes. Wise woman. By the time he turned seventeen, Rick had caught up in height, had lost his extra padding, and was lean like his friends, but more muscular. And as he trimmed down, Rick gradually chose more stylish clothes.

Few younger children, ages five through eleven, worry about their bodies. The exceptions to this are girls who begin dieting in about third grade (age 9). Although the majority of these girls are not overweight, they already show concern over their weight or size. Research estimates that, in some areas of the United States, 50 percent of all fifth-grade girls have already been on a weight-loss diet. The other kids who worry about their bodies are the ones who are obviously overweight during grade school, boys and girls alike.

Most kids go through stages of less attractiveness and even homeliness during their development. Their need for reassurance and support become greater when they feel unattractive or self-conscious about their physical flaws. These times are especially significant during the awkward periods of adolescence when kids' bodies are changing rapidly.

Teens also become much more aware of their bodies and appearance during puberty. Typical teenage concerns include hair, skin, and acne problems; weight (girls see themselves as too fat; boys, too thin), and height (too short, too tall).

Reassure your kids regularly

What can parents do to help their kids negotiate this period of sensitivity to physical imperfections? Support and reassurance can be extremely valuable. Say nothing about the obvious flaws, unless your kid brings them up. Instead, focus your attention on your kids' positive physical attributes. If your son has acne (please get the best medical help available for this), talk about his thick hair or broad shoulders. Whatever you notice that is attractive, encourage that asset and remind your son that his acne (or whatever tends to be puberty related) will improve as he gets older. If your daughter is overweight, focus on her artistic talent or her gift in science, and, of course, make sure she eats plenty of decent food throughout the day!

But what if your kids only imagine they have a problem? For example, your daughter may think she is too fat, when she clearly is not. "Don't you think I look fat in this outfit?" she may say. "I'm just a lardo!"

This is a direct request for reassurance, so don't miss it. Don't make a joke about it or lightly dismiss any concern your teens may have about their physical appearance.

Tell your daughter plainly that she is not too fat. She is just right. Get specific. Tell her she looks nice in her clothes. Tell her she is attractive or pretty. Tell her that she has a fine body. Remind her that the ultrathin models and the TV and movie stars do not have normal bodies.

Kids may act as if they don't care and don't hear you, but they are listening. And your reassurance (or your criticism) can make all the difference, for better or worse. Reassurance can ensure good self-esteem and help prevent weight and eating problems. Here's a good example:

Kari had played hockey since she was five years old. When she became a junior in high school, she was a leader on her team and considered one of the strongest skaters. There was only one problem in Kari's mind. She was convinced she had the biggest thighs in the universe. Naturally, as a skater, Kari's thighs were well developed, disproportionately large for her overall size, and they had thickened up even more since she started weight training her sophomore year. Kari's parents also had rather big thighs even though they weren't overweight either. This thigh problem affected Kari's clothes shopping, her moods, and even her self-esteem.

Several times a week Kari's parents had opportunities to reassure her that her thighs were OK and normal for her sport. She frequently complained about them and confided her worry that she'd never have a normal body, meet a nice guy, and get married—all because of her thick thighs. This talk may sound extreme and strange, but it's how teens think about their flaws sometimes. With a lot of support from her parents, Kari got through this ordeal in high school. When she finally quit hockey and weight training, her legs grew slimmer. Kari liked that, but she had learned to be OK with her thighs because her mom and dad took her concern seriously and never quit supporting her.

Offer truth to combat our culture's lies

Kids receive messages from the media, setting unattainable standards for physical size and shape. Can parents successfully combat this powerful influence? According to the statistics, it's not likely. With 75 percent of young American women reporting that they are unhappy about their shape and/or weight, so far the model-thin tomboy-shaped ideal seems to have won.

If children hear a message from their parents often enough, however, they will likely adopt it as truth. This puts a great deal of responsibility on parents, and we must be realistic about the opposition.

The American dream body and adolescent girls

Katherine Hepburn, Audrey Hepburn, and Twiggy all appeared to be naturally inclined towards ultrathinness. They all had the good fortune of sporting thin-thin figures when the culture into which they were born wanted and celebrated thin-thin females.

What has happened to American standards for beauty in the wake of these ultrathins? Twiggy launched a fashion craze from which we have not yet recovered. We in America seem to believe the adage, "You cannot be too rich or too thin." While acknowledging the first half of the statement as possibly true (although Howard Hughes comes to mind), the "can never be too thin" part has wreaked havoc among women, especially, for whom the unrealistic standards are more rigid.

This effect is steadily trickling down to our children, even into grade school, and it is a force we must reckon with.

There are two groups of kids that are probably not vulnerable to the lure of beauty and thinness standards that lead to eating avoidance:

1. Some kids are very thin genetically. They eat, they live, they don't think about it. They always maintain lightweight figures no matter what they do. They have low famine sensitivity. These are the kids, however, who are often the envy of more normal bodied kids who want to become model thin.

2. Some kids seem immune to body image struggles. They simply don't care about it. They have personalities, dispositions, and/or families, that are not given to worrying about their bodies. What a blessing! Their parents may have contributed to their security in this area, but whatever the cause, they are free of the extremely dangerous belief that "You can never be too thin."

So, what of the rest of our kids—the ones who are not immune to this message, the ones who apply the standard to their own developing bodies, the ones who try, sometimes desperately, to lower their weight even below the ideal? We're talking about kids here—eight-year-olds, nine-year-olds and all the way up to college age. How do we combat the media's bombardment on our children concerning their eating and body weight?

There is no simple answer, but we must do everything we can to help a kid who is vulnerable to these influences. Which kids are vulnerable? How can you tell?

Kids who are in danger of buying into unrealistic body-size standards

This group excludes the two groups described above: genetic thins and kids that don't care about their body weight or size. Either situation protects them from consciously interfering with their own instinctive eating. But the following are the ones we need to watch out for:

- kids, especially girls, who watch TV and go to movies
- kids who show special interest in body-focused media, such as fashion or body-building magazines
- kids involved in weight-sensitive sports, such as cheerleading, gymnastics, wrestling
- girls who experience early and/or dramatic changes at puberty
- girls whose friends are dieting.

The trouble with this American Dream Body ideal—tall, ultra-thin females and muscle-laden macho males—is that it is not ideal for most bodies, especially American-made bodies. It seems that, as the melting pot has mixed up many nationalities and races, Americans of normal size are becoming taller and larger. So most kids are simply not designed to be ultrathin, and setting up this body size as a standard for them is criminal.

These unrealistic expectations lure many kids, most of them girls, into dieting at younger and younger ages. And dieting never leads to permanent ultrathinness (with the exception of anorexia, which can be fatal) but rather to a lifetime of self-starvation dieting and temporary weight loss followed by adaptive weight gain. Girls and women actually become overweight by trying to become thinner than they were meant to be. Statistics prove that, in most cases, the more we diet, the fatter we get. So let's look at these at-risk groups a little closer.

Kids, especially girls, who watch TV or go to movies

I guess that would be all kids, or nearly all. So far, ultrathin males have not caught on as a fashion trend because ideal men are supposed to be big and strong. Big and skinny just don't mix. But boys can get a warped idea of what "normal" girls look like from these sources, and they may pressure girls to diet. Parents can help correct these unrealistic standards by pointing them out and confronting their sons' misconceptions about dieting.

But guys in general aren't nearly as vulnerable to the pervasive TV message that attractive, popular, successful females are either very thin or extremely thin. How is this message packaged to our kids? In the form of TV stars that teens are prone to idolize. So, do we attack the casting directors for picking such scrawny actresses and demand that they replace them with normal-bodied, wholesome women? The casting directors don't set the standard, but they sure help to maintain it. It's our job as parents to steer our kids away from the danger of trying to have a body like the current "star" by dieting. And the sooner we start, the better.

A balanced approach works best because anything that goes overboard with kids sets the stage for rebellion, particularly during adolescence. First, be aware of what your kids are watching on TV and watch with them at least some of the time. Look for ultrathin stars in shows they watch, and ask your kids about what they see. Talk about their observations and yours. Be careful to respect a kid's admiration for a star while honestly evaluating the body size standard.

Caroline is thirteen and never misses her favorite sit-com on Thursday nights. The four young women who star in the show are all very thin, and Caroline is just in the "bloom of womanhood." Roughly translated, that means that she is developing curvy hips and breasts. She has mentioned to her mother her concern about "getting fat." Aware of the concern, Caroline's father watches the program with her, and when it's over, they have the following conversation.

"Isn't Casey beautiful, the brunette girl with the long hair?" Caroline says. "I just love her."

"She is pretty," Dad says. "And she's a good actress, but she's too skinny for my taste."

Caroline defends her idol. "I don't think she's too skinny." (Notice her own developing standard?)

"Her body looks too much like a boy for me," her dad replies. "I think women look better with curves."

During adolescence, girls may be particularly sensitive to the "guy" point of view. Dads have power here, and a big responsibility because TV's influence is so strong.

When a college freshman was asked to explain what inspired her to diet herself into anorexia, she flatly stated, "I had to change the way I look because basically, if you go by what's on TV, you start thinking you're ugly."

Special interest in fashion or body-building magazines

Pay attention to your children's interests. If your nine-year-old daughter is buying preteen or teen magazines, leaf through them to see what she is seeing and reading. Discuss what you see. Ask her about what she sees and what she is interested in. Be honest and straightforward about the standards these models (and role models) in the magazine portray.

It's OK to make negative comments about ultrathin models while respecting your child's choice to get the publication. But if you think your daughter is especially vulnerable to the influence of the ultrathin ideal and the magazine touts this sort of thing, make it clear that the skinny models (and movie stars in general) have unrealistic figures. Tell your daughter why it is not healthy for her to try to emulate these ultrathin women by dieting or controlling her food intake, especially when she is still developing. Explain that these behaviors could either lead to eating disorders or weight gain or both.

If boys think they are too thin, they may focus on getting bigger and stronger. But this usually doesn't happen before junior high. These boys often subscribe to body-building magazines that advertise huge, muscle-bound body builders and products designed to add muscle and strength to male physiques.

Using nutritional supplements in an effort to gain muscle and bulk is usually benign and almost never results in significant weight gain. The reason is simple: Overeating, without undereating as an adaptive stress, is extremely limited as a weight-gain tactic. This is a discouraging reality to skinny adolescent boys. They can't gain no matter what they do. Age and genetics limit these teens' adaptive potential for muscle and bulk gain. This frustrates the really little or skinny guys.

How do you reassure these boys? Again, focus on the unrealistic standard set by the media. Many young boys think Mr. Universe is the ideal man in every woman's eyes. This just isn't so. Ask them about their ideals, their goals and their attitude about their body. You may be surprised at how insecure boys can feel at various stages of development.

Share your opinion about the rare "Incredible Hulk"-type bodies and the way these bodies develop—usually with the help of dangerous steroid drugs. Encourage your boys to enjoy their physical strengths (nobody has all of them), their coordination, their talent in a sport or game, or their love of the outdoors.

Kids involved in weight-sensitive sports, such as cheerleading, gymnastics, and wrestling

Sports that particularly focus on body weight can set up kids for unrealistic body-size standards. Cheerleaders and dancers may feel pressured to be as thin as the other girls they perform with. Many think they must have bodies like ultrathin movie stars, and sometimes their coaches and teachers encourage this mindset.

There are special pressures for gymnasts and wrestlers because a few pounds one way or another can interfere with performance and even eligibility. Coaches have been known to urge talented kids in these sports to do whatever it takes to keep their weight within the narrow "ideal" range for their sport. Usually these coaches don't provide healthy methods for achieving these weight requirements, so kids are left to their own devices for maintaining an optimal weight and for losing weight if they go too high. Many kids use food avoidance tactics and end up on the Feast or Famine Cycle.

Be vigilant with kids involved in these types of activities or sports. Stay alert to their eating behavior and intervene if necessary. Talk to them about their concerns, and attitudes about their bodies. Talk to their coaches about pressures they may feel. Don't be shy. When it comes to a distorted body standard, an eating disorder, or weight problem, it's easier to nip it in the bud than to fix one that has strongly taken hold.

Girls who experience early and/or dramatic changes at puberty

Children can be acutely sensitive to being different from their peers. This escalates during the teen years and accounts for the strong influence of peer pressure. Kids want to fit in, to be alike, to look alike, even to act and talk alike. But with their unique traits and unique bodies, they will likely feel the pinch of self-rejection when they change into shapes that don't fit the "norm."

When girls hit puberty, their hormones cause their bodies to change from the more angular look of childhood into the curvier shape of womanhood. Most girls welcome these changes simply as evidence of growing up. But some panic, either because their bodies change so dramatically compared with their friends that it scares them, or because they think they are getting fat. And panic precipitates desperate attempts to fix the problem—real or imagined. Because they want a fast solution, typical of teens and our society as a whole, they try extreme dieting and perhaps exhausting exercise regimens as well.

Girls who experience body-image panic during puberty need special support and reassurance. There is, for some girls, a period of "blooming" when they actually become more padded all over. If they are eating well and on time, this extra padding will gradually wane as they move into their late teens and early twenties. Parents can reassure them about their bodies and encourage them to keep eating good food whenever they get hungry. Without support, reassurance and helpful information about instinctive eating, these girls are sitting ducks for the Feast or Famine Cycle and all the trouble it brings.

Girls whose friends are dieting

Dieting has become such a way of life in this country that our kids are doing it just to fit in! Girls are vulnerable to dieting even though they have no weight problem and are not worried about their weight. They may get caught in the trap simply because their group of friends is dieting. They do it to be accepted. They want to be one of the thin ones if they aren't already, *or really thin* if they're genetically slim. The goal is to stay far away from the danger zone of being labeled fat. As disturbing as it sounds, kids can bond through a common goal, such as losing weight and eating as little as possible.

Peer pressure pushes kids to fit in by doing what their friends are doing. That's how they feel accepted. Unless children and teens are educated about the dangers of traditional eat-less dieting, they fall prey to this influence. It's amazing that kids who clearly have no weight problem at all will attempt to lose weight simply because it's the "in" thing to do. Most parents don't realize the danger of this peer-inspired behavior because they don't see how destructive limiting food intake can be.

For some kids, short-term dieting doesn't have obvious negative consequences—at least not in the immediate future. But for others, it is the beginning of the end of their instinctive relationship with food and the freedom to eat the way they were designed to eat.

Eat-less, exercise-more dieting is still in vogue after fifty years

According to the latest statistics on obesity, we are nation of mostly fat people. Being overweight, if not obese, is the norm in the United States in the twenty-first century. This is a fact. We are not only a nation of fat people, we are a nation of dieters—people trying all kinds of ways to eat less food on a regular basis. *There is a positive correlation here*, and we have been missing it so far. Methods for weight loss are legion in our country. The diet industry is worth over thirty billion dollars a year.

More than 95 percent of dieters have not accomplished permanent weight loss through the eat-less, exercise-more approach. In fact it is making us fatter.

But we keep believing it. And we keep infecting our kids with it too. How can they help but get caught up in the same trap that so many of their parents are caught in—especially when our culture idolizes body sizes for women and men that are only approachable by perhaps 5 percent of the population?

Prevention of obesity and eating disorders

If we are going to turn the tide on this epidemic in our country, we must start with our kids—preferably *before* they have developed a weight or eating problem. But even before that, we must start with our own enlightenment about these problems:

Obesity and eating disorders are not caused by simple choices, and they cannot be solved by quick and simple solutions. They are caused by patterns of eating avoidance and make-up eating, undereating and overeating.

The problems of obesity and eating disorders are complex, and if we are to prevent them, we must understand them in their complexity. We need to see why people make choices that lead to weight and eating problems. Only then can we light a path for our kids to follow.

Remember, the three ways adults can protect their kids are modeling, education and support.

Modeling: Apply the principles of responsible, instinctive eating to your own life.

Education: Yours is happening to you now, as you read. You educate your children as you discuss these topics and begin making schedule and food-choice changes. Reread this book and underline the important concepts. Dog-ear the pages. Review. It's so important to get a hold of the

Naturally Thin principles because it's a whole new way of thinking, generally at odds with the messages we get from the media and our friends. You have to understand the principles well enough to teach them to your kids and consistently reinforce them.

Support: Teaching kids to eat good food on time and reinforcing body-controlled eating behavior is essential for kids who live in a world of eat-less, eat-on-the-run, no-time-to-eat messages.

You can give them a great gift to last a lifetime: freedom from struggles with food and obesity.

Do your best.

Looking to the future

This book focuses on individual parents and kids' caretakers who want to improve their kids' chances of enjoying a healthy weight and normal eating patterns for life. Broader cultural change can only be inspired by enlightened individuals.

Here are some important broader goals we can work toward:

- making affordable quality breakfast foods available before school for all school-age children
- raising the quality of school lunch menus and eliminating poor-quality food options
- integrating snack times into the mid-morning school schedule
- eliminating poor-quality foods, such as soda pop and candy bars, from school cafeterias, or making them unavailable during lunchtime
- making sure day-care menus for meals and snacks meet high-quality standards
- educating school sports coaches about the importance of making quality food available to all players for practices and games with help from parents

- lobbying to ensure that fast-food chains will not be granted government contracts to supply food for school children unless these chains develop high-quality products for school menus
- integrating into the school day ample recess periods specifically for physical free play for all grade school children
- making physical education classes mandatory again for all kids, kindergarten through high school
- requiring all high school students to complete a health class in which they learn the principles of body-controlled eating and good nutrition
- conducting parenting classes that include instruction in body-controlled eating and food quality.

These are lofty goals. Some may seem out of reach because we have gotten so far off track. But the starting point toward achieving these goals is right in your kitchen, on your grocery list, in your new understanding. A long journey begins with a single step, a book begins with a word, and a revolution begins with a new idea.

Appendix

Snack ideas

All snacks may be made with any combination of real foods. These are examples of the most common ingredients in real-food snacks:

peanut butter
breads, bagels, English muffins, tortillas
crackers and cheese
cheese and cut-up fruit
cottage cheese with fruit
yogurt
nuts
cut-up vegetables with dip
fruit
apples with peanut butter
ants on a log (celery filled with peanut butter, topped with raisins)
soup
sandwiches
salads
cereals
granola or protein bars
milkshakes with fruit (smoothies)
meal leftovers
jelly, honey

Breakfast ideas

cold cereal, preferably with nuts and fruit, milk, buttered toast
toasted sandwiches with ham and/or cheese, fruit juice or milk
eggs cooked any way, toast, juice
toasted bread or English muffins with peanut butter or cream cheese, hot chocolate

pizza, milk or fruit juice
waffles, bacon or ham, milk
oatmeal with cream, nuts, and raisins, toast, milk

Hearty breakfasts can keep kids' energy and attention levels high until lunchtime. The best way to ensure that your kids will stay satisfied throughout the morning is to include protein foods and fat in their breakfasts.

Lunch ideas

turkey or beef sandwich with cole slaw
grilled cheese sandwich with soup
grilled chicken roll-ups (leftover chicken) with potato salad
pizza, (leftover or freshly baked), lettuce salad
macaroni and cheese with veggies and dip
lasagna (leftover) and green beans with garlic bread
tuna salad sandwich or tuna melt with fruit
tacos and refried beans

Dinner ideas

spaghetti, salad, garlic bread
chicken breast sandwiches, green beans, coleslaw
steak, broccoli, baked potatoes
pork chops or tofu stir-fry with rice
eggs and fried potatoes, baked beans
grilled cheese sandwiches, tomato soup, veggies with dip
stew with bread and butter
pizza, salad
macaroni and cheese, three-bean salad
chili, crackers or bread

The goal for a balanced meal is to combine these three groups:

meat or fish or poultry or vegetable protein
   with
vegetables and/or fruits
   and
bread/rice/potato/pasta/legume.

Additional tips

Keep fruits and vegetables on hand and offer them with every meal. Put vegetables your kids like, such as lettuce, tomato, sprouts, and cucumbers, on sandwiches and in rollups. Be creative. Some kids like peanut butter and banana sandwiches, others fried egg sandwiches with catsup.

Milk is the most nutritious beverage but 100 percent fruit juices are fine too. Always offer water because your kids may not think of it and it is a good option.

These are fairly typical American dishes, but ethnic foods can also qualify as real foods. Don't worry about getting every food group into every meal, but offer a spectrum of foods from each food group throughout the day. The five basic food groups roughly divide the real food list:

- breads and grains, (pasta, rice, potatoes, legumes, nuts)
- fruits and vegetables
- dairy, (eggs, milk, cheese, yogurt)
- meats, poultry, seafood, and vegetarian protein products such as tofu
- fats (butter, oil, salad dressings).

Fast Facts

Obesity among children (ages 6-11) and adolescents (ages 12-19) has more than doubled between 1976 and 2000.
American Obesity Association, 2001. Childhood Obesity, Prevalence and Identification

Prevalence and trends in overweight among US children and adolescents, 1999-2000.
Ogden, Flegal, Carroll MD, Johnson

Nearly two-thirds of adults in the US are overweight and over 30 percent are obese.
National Health and Nutrition Examination Survey, 1999-2000

Childhood obesity on the Rise: The doubling of obesity statistics is in both children and adolescents and in all age, race, and gender groups.
Carol Torgan, PhD., National Institutes of Health, June 2002

The age–adjusted prevalence of combined overweight and obesity in racial/ethnic minorities—especially women—is generally higher than in whites in the US.
National Health and Nutrition Examination Survey, 1999-2000

Eating disorders affect 10 percent of college students, mostly women . . .and body dissatisfaction and desire to lose weight are the norm for more than 70 percent of young women in the US. Some studies estimate the rate of bulimia among college students as high as 20 percent. That's one woman in five.
Harvard University and Radcliffe College study, 2001

Studies report that 95-98% of people who lose weight [by

dieting] gain it back within five years. 90% of those gain back more weight than they lost. Only 2-5% of dieters succeed in keeping their weight off. The failure of weight loss programs is so great that a leading researcher has said, "Dieting is the leading cause of obesity in the US."

National Institutes of Health

The annual revenue for the diet industry in the US was over 30 billion dollars in 1990.

Marketdata Enterprises

The average US fashion model is 5'9" to 6' tall and weighs 110-118 pounds and is seventeen to twenty-six years old. These models wear a size 6-8 dress. The average American woman is 5'4" to 5'5" tall, weighs 142 pounds, wears size 14 and is 44 years old.

National Health Statistics, 2001

Girls who perceive their mothers as frequently trying to lose weight were more likely to develop into chronic dieters them-selves.

Dr. Alison Field and colleagues at Brigham and Women's Hospital, Boston, The journal, "Pediatrics," January, 2001

Fewer than one in five children eats the recommended five servings a day of fruits and vegetables, and more than 60 percent consume more fat than is recommended.

Centers for Disease Control and Prevention

Describes the connection between lipoprotein lipase levels and fat storage and also found that dieting (undereating) creates cravings for calorie-dense mixtures of sugar and fat.

Dr. Adam Drewnowski, Ph.D.,director of human nutrition, University of Michigan at Ann Arbor, 1991

Research with starved normal weight volunteers shows that this condition is accompanied by general apathy, depression, and total preoccupation with food, the same symptoms reported by chronic dieters.

Keys, Brozeck, Henschel, Mickelson, and Taylor, 1950

Basal metabolism accounts for a majority of total energy expenditure. Caloric restriction produces a 15% to30% decrease in basal metabolic rate in all persons.

Kelly Brownell, professor of psychology at Yale University, referencing Apfelbaum et al., 1971; Bray, 1969; Drenick & Dennin, 1973; Kroikewski, Sjostrom, & Sullivan, 1977

Obesity appears to be highly heritable, as determined by studies of twins and adoptees. If neither parent is obese, the likelihood of the child's becoming obese is only 8%. If one parent is obese, the likelihood jumps to 40%, and if both parents are overweight, the probability of the child's becoming obese is an astonishing 80%.

Foch & McLearn, 1980

Index

A
activity
See also athletics; exercise; recess avoidance, problems of, 26, 30, 147
calorie conservation and, 46
delayed eating and, 37, 42
dieting/fasting and, 27
famine and, 60–61, 91
food availability and, 59
overweight and, 138, 147
physical education, 182
recommendations, 149
result of feasting phase, 43
adaptation
adaptive potential, 35
adaptive responses, 21, 25–31
famine and, 41–42, 138, 157
Feast or Famine Cycle and, 40, 43, 156
genetics and, 46
strength of, 42
adolescents
See also puberty/adolescence; cultural messages
exercise and, 148
father's influence on daughters, 175
food availability and, 144
growth spurts and body changes, 19, 169
insecurity, 167
risks for weight and eating problems, 27
American Dream Body, 172, 173
anorexia nervosa, 93, 174, 175
appetite(s), 29, 94, 109
loss of, 112
suppression, 160
antidepressants, 47
athletics, 21, 31, 39
hunger needs and, 79, 87, 121–122, 136–139, 140, 181
mesomorphic body types and, 65–67
overweight and, 60
weight-sensitive sports, 173, 177